# GOING BLUE

## a TEEN GUIDE to SAVING our OCEANS, LAKES, RIVERS, & WETLANDS

by **Cathryn Berger Kaye, M.A.,**
with **Philippe Cousteau**
& **EarthEcho International**

**Library of Congress Cataloging-in-Publication Data**
Kaye, Cathryn Berger.
  Going blue : a teen guide to saving our oceans & waterways / by Cathryn Berger Kaye ; with Philippe Cousteau and EarthEcho International.
       p. cm.
  Includes bibliographical references and index.
  ISBN 978-1-57542-348-7
  1. Marine ecology. 2. Marine pollution—Prevention. 3. Environmentalism. I. Cousteau, Philippe. II. Title.
  QH541.5.S3K4 2010
  333.91'16—dc22

                                                                                    2010016589

Free Spirit Publishing does not have control over or assume responsibility for author or third-party websites and their content. At the time of this book's publication, all facts and figures cited within are the most current available. All telephone numbers, addresses, and website URLs are accurate and active; all publications, organizations, websites, and other resources exist as described in this book; and all have been verified as of April 2010. If you find an error or believe that a resource listed here is not as described, please contact Free Spirit Publishing. Parents, teachers, and other adults: We strongly urge you to monitor children's use of the Internet.

Service learning occurs in each of the fifty United States and internationally. Some project descriptions are attributed to specific schools or youth groups and identified by city, state, or region. All efforts have been made to ensure correct attribution. Some of the names of the young people quoted throughout the book have been changed to protect their privacy.

Reading Level Grades 6 & up; Interest Level Ages 11 & up;
Fountas & Pinnell Guided Reading Level Y

Edited by Meg Bratsch
Cover and interior design by Tasha Kenyon

Text on pages 86 & 88 is adapted from the article "Our Blue Planet: Ocean Exploration" by Charles H. McLaughlin Jr. *Technology and Children*. December 1, 2005. Copyright © 2009 International Technology Education Association. Used with permission.

10 9 8 7 6 5 4 3 2
Printed in The United States of America
U19810710

**Free Spirit Publishing Inc.**
217 Fifth Avenue North, Suite 200
Minneapolis, MN 55401-1299
(612) 338-2068
help4kids@freespirit.com
www.freespirit.com

Free Spirit Publishing is a member of the Green Press Initiative, and we're committed to printing our books on recycled paper containing a minimum of 30% post-consumer waste (PCW). For every ton of books printed on 30% PCW recycled paper, we save 5.1 trees, 2,100 gallons of water, 114 gallons of oil, 18 pounds of air pollution, 1,230 kilowatt hours of energy, and .9 cubic yards of landfill space. At Free Spirit it's our goal to nurture not only young people, but nature too!

VOC
FREE

**Printed on recycled paper**
including 30%
post-consumer waste

green
press
INITIATIVE

# Dedication

From Cathryn: "To all the young people who transform ideas into saving this water planet. And to my father, James David Berger, who first introduced me to our oceans."

From Philippe: "To my mother, who inspired me to dedicate my life to making this world a better place."

# Acknowledgments

This book grew through the contributions of many. Our appreciation goes to all who gave their time, stories, and words to fill these pages. With special gratitude to:

- EarthEcho International—Mia DeMezza, Kyra Kristof, and Nicole Ross—for the collaboration, knowledge, and joy you brought to this endeavor.

- Free Spirit Publishing, especially Judy Galbraith for her excitement and Meg Bratsch for her editing skills.

- Jane Goodall's Roots & Shoots and Youth Service America for assistance with international service learning stories.

- George Buckley and his students at the Sustainability and Environmental Management Program, Harvard University Extension School, for their research contributions.

- Lance Morgan at Marine Conservation Biology Institute for his thorough scientific review.

- Sachiko Cooper DaSilva, Nate Ivy, Rebecca Jim, Dave Makepeace, Nan Peterson, Jon Schmidt, Adelaide Schwartz, and Yvonne Whittaker for great examples.

- Our "movers & shakers"—Alexandra Cousteau and Alex Lin—for living the courage of your convictions.

- Writers Raj Mundra for permission to excerpt his article "Niswarth in Mumbai," Carlyn Tani for permission to excerpt her article "Mokule'ia Campers Help Preserve Ka'ena Point," and Charles McLaughlin for permission to excerpt his article "Our Blue Planet: Ocean Exploration."

From Cathryn: "I would like to thank my husband Barry for his patience with my late writing hours and my daughters Devora and Ariel—all of whom give me encouragement and love that inspires me daily."

# Contents

# What Teens Think About Saving Our Oceans, Lakes, Rivers, & Wetlands

"People see the awesome power of the ocean and think it is indestructible. I believe that ocean life needs to be protected, and since oceans are all connected, our efforts have to be global to be successful."—Ian, age 16

"For me, the oceans were all about going to the beach . . . until I found out about that mass of plastic floating in the Pacific. Where my trash goes matters. I can do something about this."—Rhea, age 15

"We need to care about our environment *now* to help us survive on Earth. We need the oxygen from trees, the clean water, and the healthy air that we get from taking care of what we have."—Evan, age 14

"If we use up all of our natural resources, there will be no more and then the world will be in chaos. To start, kids can pick up garbage by the water and make signs and banners to warn people about what will happen if they throw garbage away carelessly."—Nabil, age 14

"Think of all of the things that live in our water—the animals, the plants, the bacteria, the bugs. They are all living creatures like us so they deserve to live just as much as we do. Imagine you lived in the water and one day a giant dumped a bunch of oil in it, and everything around you dies, and then finally you die, too. See what I'm talking about?"—Maddie, age 13

"Protecting our oceans and waterways is important because if they get polluted, our culture could drastically change. The environment would become our first priority, and we'd have to set aside some of the other, equally important things such as world peace. If we protect our waterways now, we are protecting our entire society."—Jude, age 15

"The work we do today is important for future generations. We may not see much effect in our lifetime, but we know our children will."—Kiddest, age 17

# A Call to Action from Philippe Cousteau

Philippe Cousteau is the cofounder of the ocean conservation and education organization EarthEcho International and grandson of the legendary ocean explorer Jacques Cousteau. In this interview he explains why now is the time—more than ever—to become an environmental champion.

My grandfather's first adventures into the world at large were considerably different than the ones we embark on today. He was one of the first people to explore the oceans—his was a true journey of discovery. Few, if any, had seen the wonders of the deep captured on film. Jacques Cousteau and his crew were the first to capture those images and share them with the wider world. Imagine all the creatures we have grown up with and take for granted—from coral reefs to polar bears, Nemo the clownfish and even Shamu the whale. All were total mysteries to the world.

I encourage you to watch two films my grandfather produced many years ago. *The Silent World* and *World Without Sun* won Academy Awards and showcase Jacques Cousteau and my father Philippe Cousteau Sr. diving the reefs off the coast of Southern France and the Red Sea in the 1950s and 60s and filming them for the first time in human history.

My father, Philippe Cousteau Sr., passed away in an airplane accident six months before I was born. Growing up with tales of his adventures, I heard stories of how he took his first breath underwater and descended to those reefs. I was told of his devastation at seeing what happened to those very same reefs, now mere shadows of what they once were, due to climate change and pollution. I spent many hours of my own youth diving off the coast of France and I can no longer stand to go back. I find the barren, desolate underwater landscape so terrible. It can break your heart when you see the beauty captured by my grandfather on film and know that today that beauty is virtually gone.

As part of the third Cousteau generation, I see my role as a journey to understand the relationship between humans and nature, and especially to be a steward of this planet. Of course I am proud to have the Cousteau name. But I'm not a Cousteau only because of my name. The Cousteau spirit of conservation and care for the environment was taught to me. It lives on through me because of my actions, not my birth certificate.

Daily, I consider the choices I make and the influence I can have by sharing information and ideas with others. Of the many concerns facing our environment, without question, the excessive output of carbon into the atmosphere is the most troubling. Carbon is the leading cause of climate change. This current global crisis is changing our oceans—the primary drivers of our climate.

As climate changes, the domino effects will be felt around the world. For example, water scarcity will likely be the defining cause of conflict and mass migration of people in the 21st century. In large part this will be instigated by the world's changing weather patterns brought about by changing currents and rising temperatures and sea levels in the ocean—all caused by climate change. That is a bit of a simplification, but you get the idea: everything is connected to everything else on this planet.

But climate change isn't the only problem caused by carbon. The excessive output of carbon into the atmosphere is also responsible for another very scary problem that has nothing to do with climate change: ocean acidification. OA, as we call it, is caused purely by the absorption of carbon by the oceans. The carbon absorption causes oceans to become more acidic and ocean creatures that build shells—such as coral, shellfish, mollusks, and pteropods (small free swimming snails that form the basis of many ocean food chains)—are unable to build shells and survive. If this continues, the wholesale collapse

> "The Cousteau spirit of conservation and care for the environment was taught to me. It lives on through me because of my actions, not my birth certificate."

of many ocean ecosystems will have disastrous effects on the planet. Imagine: more than a billion people currently rely on fish for their primary source of protein. If fisheries collapse because they have no basic food source, those people would starve and many would go to war to feed themselves. That is just one example; others are just as serious.

If this seems pretty depressing, remember: there is hope. The key to helping these creatures survive is to give them the healthiest, safest environments in which to live. For example, coral reefs in a pristine environment are much more likely to adapt to rising water temperatures than those already stressed from pollution and overfishing. That is good news, and it means that we must double our efforts to protect our environment.

Some of the most effective solutions involve replacing the exploitation of natural resources with alternatives that protect our environment and have mutual benefits. In Florida during the 1990s, gill net fishing (a very destructive form of fishing) was banned along the coast. Instead of putting the gill net fishermen out of work, scientists devised a way for them to grow clams in baskets along the shore. This simple form of aquaculture was even more lucrative than gill net fishing and it protected the environment. In a short period of time, Florida went from being last in clam production in the United States to being first.

> "Remember: there is hope. The key to helping these creatures survive is to give them the healthiest, safest environments in which to live. . . . We must double our efforts to protect our environment."

We have a chance to change this world. The last 50 years have seen the greatest amount of destruction on this planet in history, and it is the next 50 years—our 50 years—that will decide its fate. This means demanding that our politicians take these problems seriously by expressing a willingness to make changes in our own lives. Ask yourself: "Do I really need a bigger house or a bigger car?" A comfortable life is what we all aspire to, that is human nature. However, a comfortable life could be defined by living in gracious and sustainable harmony with the planet. Each of you has an exciting opportunity to consider what choices you will make and what distinct steps you will take to be part of both a local and a global solution.

You probably hear people tell you all the time that you can make a difference. But the truth is this: You already make a difference. *Everything you do makes a difference.* Every single one of your actions has consequences. What do you want to be the results of the actions you take every single day? Look around at the world you live in—this time with "super-vision"—to see deeper into the impact of each choice. What can you be doing?

Start with simple things, like bringing reusable bags when you shop, finding an area in your community to protect, being "water smart" at every opportunity, and encouraging your parents to vote for politicians who care about your future. Endless reports prove the number one reason adults change their behavior is because of the influence of their children . . . you have *power!*

> "You probably hear people tell you all the time that you can make a difference. But the truth is this: *Everything you do makes a difference. . . .* What do you want to be the results of the actions you take every single day?"

I grew up sitting with my grandfather and listening to his life's stories, hearing the urgency in his voice, being inspired by the passion my own father had for taking action for a better future. Their voices influenced me in becoming the person I am today. You could call it a family legacy, or just good teaching. Regardless, I am a firm believer that if we are to build the sustainable future we all dream of, we must do it together. Each of us—*all* of us—making a positive difference; that is a legacy we can all share.

Philippe Cousteau

# What Do You Know?

1. "Water has no beginning, end, or middle."
   What does this statement mean?

2. What fraction of the earth is covered by water?

3. Which of the following does the ocean provide: oxygen, rain, food, or oil?

4. What percentage of the oceans has been explored: 5%, 25%, 50%, or 85%?

5. Which of your everyday activities affect our oceans?

Have you thought about our oceans and **waterways** lately? Perhaps you've seen headlines about polluted lakes, toxic rivers, droughts, waterborne illnesses, rising sea levels, or coral reef damage. These days more ocean species are considered endangered than ever, and human overfishing threatens to starve dolphins, sharks, and seabirds. During the summer of 2009, the world's ocean temperatures were the warmest ever recorded. New lakes and rivers are being added to endangered lists yearly. In many countries, drought has dried up food crops and safe drinking water is difficult to find.

The term **waterways** (as used in this book) includes all bodies of water on Earth apart from oceans—from ground springs to streams, brooks, creeks, ponds, marshes, wetlands, lakes, rivers, canals, bays, lagoons, ice fields, and seas.

We have depended upon our waters since the dawn of life on this planet. They feed us, quench our thirst, help us travel and transport goods, provide medicine, create energy, and let us swim, surf, sail, and dream. However, these same waters are changing in ways that threaten our way of life now and for future generations. Our oceans and waterways are hurting. With increasing acidification in the oceans, glaciers melting at the poles, and trash accumulating everywhere, what we have taken for granted for too long needs to be addressed. And *fast*.

The good news is that we can do something. We can step in, learn about the issues that are all interconnected—just like our waterways—and create plans for action. We can talk with others, find out what is already being done in our communities, regions, and nations, and join in. We can come up with brand new ideas to meet the water needs we see around us every day.

You've probably heard the phrase "going green," which means pitching in to help the environment—our forests, fields, land, and air. This remains essential. What this book proposes is to add another color to the mix by going *blue* and helping to conserve and protect our planet's water. What can you do to go blue?

> "We all have to take responsibility for the direction we are going. In our schools we need, from the earliest times, to get across the concept that we are connected to nature and that we are trying to find a space to sustain ourselves."
>
> —*Sylvia Earle, oceanographer*

## Starting Now

However you found this book or it found you, these pages will help you discover ways to address community or global problems. Whatever you choose to do to help our oceans and waterways—whether it's organizing a water usage awareness campaign, cleaning a local creek, planting trees to stop soil erosion, or eating more locally grown food—the time to start is *now*.

### Did You Get the Right Answers?

Here are the answers to the questions on page 6. Our oceans and waterways are all interconnected and flow without beginning, middle, or end. A full three-fourths of the earth is covered by water, making ours truly a "water planet." Our oceans provide all four of these things: oxygen, rain, food, and oil. Only 5 percent of our oceans have been explored by humans, which leaves plenty for you to do! And every single one of your daily activities affects our oceans and waterways—from the electronics you use, to the clothes you put on, to the foods you eat. By reading on, you will find out exactly how these choices and others reach to the furthest depths of the ocean.

# What's Inside?

This book is filled with curious questions, eye-opening facts, useful information, inspiring quotes, amazing photos, extraordinary stories, and plenty of examples of what teens just like you are doing to keep this planet of ours healthy. All of this information is divided according to the five stages of an exciting journey called *service learning*. These five stages are **Investigation**, **Preparation**, **Action**, **Reflection**, and **Demonstration** (each stage is explained in detail in the next chapter). You'll also notice four repeating sections throughout the book: The **Teens in Action** sections tell recent stories of real teens across the world making significant contributions. The **Your Turn** boxes help you relate the topics discussed to your own life and give you ideas for getting involved. The **Time for Reflection** boxes ask questions that encourage you to pause, think, and look at the larger picture of what you are doing. And the **EarthEcho** boxes suggest tips for how to transform the information and ideas that you read here into simple day-to-day actions that benefit the planet.

# How to Read This Book

There is no one "right" way to read this book. You might decide to plunge in and read it straight through, from beginning to end. Or you can pick and choose sections that interest you at a given time, or that relate directly to a service plan you already have in progress. To help navigate whichever route you choose, each of the five service learning stages is introduced with an example of what actual teens did at that stage during a specific service learning experience (see **The Story of Tar Creek, Parts #1–5**, beginning on page 18), and each stage ends with a box briefly summarizing its contents.

Beware that once you dive in, there may be no returning to the surface. You may realize it's time to change the tide and reclaim your water planet. You may feel compelled to join in the challenge to investigate, explore, brainstorm, plan, and get involved to improve your world. You may find yourself a changed person. You may even find yourself turning a little . . . *blue.*

## Tips for Using this Book

- You are holding a written guide, but you will find other guides around you—adults you meet who know about our waters, friends, family, and community members who are all eager to help. People all across the globe are getting involved every day. Ask them questions. Learn what they have to share.

- Use a journal (made of recycled or reused paper) to keep track of your thoughts and observations as you read.

- Stay informed about current news involving our oceans and waterways, including issues of climate change and global warming.

- Visit the many websites listed in this book to find additional information and resources.

- Involve others in your journey—friends, family, a class, or a youth group. Learn, think, laugh, and work together to get the job done.

- Let your creativity inspire you to be an agent of change. Planet Earth needs **you.**

# Service + Learning = Service Learning

What is service learning and how does it fit into all of this? Simple: service learning is the adventure that will take you from where you are now . . . to where you will be—helping rescue our planet's water by using your knowledge, skills, interests, energy, and enthusiasm. Service + Learning = a recipe for action and success. This chapter introduces you to the process of service learning, and along the way provides examples of what you can do at each of its stages.

Service: Service means contributing to or helping to benefit others and the common good.

Learning: Learning means gaining an understanding of a subject or developing a skill through study, experience, or an exchange of ideas.

Service Learning: The ideas of service and learning combine to create service learning. Investigation, preparation, action, reflection, and demonstration are the five stages of service learning. By understanding how each stage works, you can be more effective in making plans to help in your community and the world.

## Stage 1: Find Out → Investigate

"People can only protect what they love, but they can only love what they know."—Philippe Cousteau Sr., explorer

The journey of service learning begins the way you begin many things: you **investigate**. What do you investigate? First, you investigate the resources that you bring to helping this planet. Then, you investigate the needs in your community related to oceans and waterways.

**YOUR TURN** ➤ **Create an Inventory of Your Skills and Talents.** Do you enjoy photography, writing, art, research, math, or science? Are you a behind-the-scenes organizer or do you prefer being onstage with a microphone? Throughout service learning, your interests and abilities can be further developed. Stretch your mind as you think of all your skills and talents. If you are exploring *Going Blue* with a friend, interview each other to discover skills and talents. Ask questions. Make an inventory—a list—and keep it visible as you prepare, act on, demonstrate, and reflect on your ideas. This inventory can be helpful at every stage of your voyage. Remember, every person has unique value.

**What Community Needs Interest You?** Start a list and then discuss it with others and let your list grow. What topics are of greatest interest to people you speak with? Which ones capture the attention of just a few? Here's a surprise: Nearly every community need you can think of will have something to do with water. As you read on, you will find out how.

## Investigation Example: Water Audit

Sometimes a community need appears in the form of a question. That happened when one middle school student asked: "How much water do we use?" This led her class to the challenging task of investigating and evaluating water usage at their school and in their homes. Were they wasting water? How could they find out? What could they do about it?

The students learned to read water bills and took a walking tour of their school to identify ways to conserve water. They developed a survey for home use to record how much water each family member used per week. They compared the results with the average water use in the United States of 80 to 100 gallons each day. After hearing a guest speaker describe strategies for water reduction at home, and conducting research through books and the Internet, students created and distributed a family-friendly guide, *Save Water: We Need Every Drop.*

Reread the previous paragraph. What skills and talents did the students put to use? What techniques did they use to investigate the community need? This will help you begin to investigate water issues in your own community.

# Stage 2: Dive In → Prepare

**"It takes as much energy to wish as it does to plan."**
—Eleanor Roosevelt, former first lady of the United States, author, humanitarian

The next step on the service learning journey is to *prepare*. You have experience preparing all the time. You prepare for school in the morning, you prepare for a basketball game by shooting hoops, you learn lines for a play, and you gather ingredients to bake cookies.

## Preparation Example: Flood Readiness

Imagine that your community experiences severe flooding. The flood might be due to a storm, to problems with overdevelopment, to soil erosion, or to some other cause. After investigating the issue, you decide to find ways to help people in your community know what to do if flooding occurs again. How would you prepare to help your community be ready for a flooding disaster? Answer this question on your own first, *before* reading the list below.

Now look at this list. Did you have similar ideas?

- Talk to people who work for emergency relief services, such as the Red Cross. Find out what they require for a flooding emergency. Do they need common supplies that could be collected, like blankets? What do they suggest people do to prepare for a flood?

- Speak to rescue workers, such as paramedics or firefighters. Are local maps accurate enough for them to reach the most remote homes in your community?

- Interview community members who were affected by past floods. What advice do they have about preparedness?

- Visit the location where people have been relocated during past floods, such as a school gymnasium or community center. What would make this place more welcoming—for adults, children, and pets—if it is needed again for this purpose?

- Read about the causes of flooding in your community and what can be done to prevent it. Educating the community about flood awareness could be part of your action plan.

- Check out local newspaper coverage of recent floods. Who in your local government has ideas and knowledge about the issue? Can you meet with this person?

Part of preparation is finding people and organizations that care about the community need you've chosen to address. Gather the contact information for these people and build a team that can help you plan. This includes brainstorming ideas and generating possibilities. Think big and wide—all of this preparation and planning leads to the next stage of service learning . . .

# Stage 3: Get Going → Act

"If you're walking down the right path and you're willing to keep walking, eventually you'll make progress."—Barack Obama, United States President

Once you have investigated your interests, skills, and community needs, and are prepared with the background knowledge you need, you are ready to create and carry out a plan to **act**. Action typically occurs as direct service, indirect service, advocacy, research, or a combination of several of these approaches.

**Direct Service:** Your service involves face-to-face interactions or close contact with people, animals, or the environment—such as rivers, lakes, oceans, or any part of the watershed that is near you.

**Indirect Service:** Your action is not seen by the people or animals who may benefit from it, but it meets a real need.

**Advocacy:** What you do makes others aware of an issue and encourages them to take action to change a situation.

**Research:** You gather and report on information that helps a community.

## Action Example: Flood Readiness

Using the scenario of flood readiness again, here are examples of the different types of action that students have taken.

**Direct Service:** Students organized books, games, and toys and placed them in bins to be stored in the school gymnasium for use in flooding emergencies. They would then be able to lead activities with young children, entertain pets, and help families cope with the difficult situation.

**Indirect Service:** In case of flooding and evacuation, what documents must a family take with them? Students prepared large envelopes with a list of all the necessary documents—birth records, insurance papers, medical information, pet information—that families can place inside and take with them in case of an emergency evacuation.

**Advocacy:** A youth group learned how commercial development had caused soil erosion, leading to increased risks of flooding. They worked with local politicians to hold a town forum to discuss local concerns and advocate for zoning to protect fragile areas.

**Research:** Using photography, video, and podcasts, students documented the experiences and effects of flooding in their community and compiled a report for response teams and civic groups.

**Four Action Strategies**
What if you wanted to address toxic dumping in your local waterways? Think of an example for each of these four types of action.

## Stage 4: Think Back ➞ Reflect

"The most important thing is to actually think about what you do. To become aware and actually think about the effect of what you do on the environment and on society. That's key, and that underlies everything else."—Jane Goodall, environmentalist

What is one piece of information you have learned so far that you want to remember? What is one idea you have now that you didn't have before opening this book? When you answer these questions, you *reflect*: you look at your experience to determine what it has to do with you. Reflection takes place all along the service learning journey: as you investigate and prepare, as you do the service, and as you demonstrate what you have learned and accomplished. You will find reflection built into this book in the **Time for Reflection** boxes and in a series of questions in the Reflection section on pages 128–129.

## Stage 5: Tell It → Demonstrate

"Not only is your story worth telling, but it can be told in words so painstakingly eloquent that it becomes a song."—Gloria Naylor, novelist and educator

In this final stage you review what you learned, how you planned, what you did, and how you've reflected along the way. Then you tell others; you **demonstrate**. Here, you can again draw upon your interests and abilities to showcase your service learning efforts. How you tell your story is up to you. Will you:

*Make a mural?*

*Create a website?*

*Build a display for your school or town hall?*

*Produce a PowerPoint presentation?*

*Perform a skit for a class or youth group?*

*Record a video or podcast?*

*Write an article for a school or community newspaper?*

*Create a comic book or brochure showing the steps you took?*

*Going Blue* guides you through the service learning journey as you investigate, prepare, act, reflect, and demonstrate—all toward saving our oceans and waterways. So let's get started!

# STAGE 1
## FIND OUT → INVESTIGATE

In this first stage of your service learning journey, you will take steps to find out more about yourself and your skills and about the community you are trying to help. You will learn about the issues and identify a water-related need that you want to address.

# The Story of Tar Creek: Part #1
## Miami, Oklahoma, United States

Brownish orange in color, Tar Creek stretches across the northeastern tip of Oklahoma, a region suffering from almost a century of lead and zinc mining that has left behind a mess of residue. Starting here with Investigation (Stage 1), you will follow the story of Tar Creek through the Five Stages of Service Learning.

Imagine seeing mountains of toxic waste wherever you looked. Students in Miami, Oklahoma, actually live in these surroundings, where mining waste has poisoned their land, water, and air. In fact, their community is so badly polluted it has been identified as a **Superfund site**. At the local high school, the students and their school counselor, Rebecca Jim, took the challenge of educating the community about their hazardous surroundings—including Tar Creek, one of the most polluted bodies of water in the United States. They have since become knowledgeable advocates determined to save their community.

> A **Superfund site** is identified by the Environmental Protection Agency as a place where toxic waste has been dumped and needs to be cleaned up. About 600,000 toxic waste sites exist across the United States. One out of four people in the United States lives within four miles of a Superfund site.

**How Did They Investigate?**

The initial group of students who took on the Tar Creek challenge used various means of research to uncover the need. They documented their observations with photography and personal stories; they mapped areas that seemed most impacted. They studied the history of mining in the area to root out the causes of the toxicity. They interviewed local ranchers and community elders to gather accounts of what they have seen and experienced over time. Based on this rich evidence, students established a real need: community awareness to prevent exposure to Tar Creek polluted water and other waste from mining.

The Story of Tar Creek continues on page 60.

**Tar Creek Superfund site.** Photo credit: Janice Curtis

# Getting Started:
## Your Water, Your Community, Your World

What needs to be uncovered about water in your community? Become a detective and find out what you need to know.

## Get Active in Your Research

Have you ever received an assignment to do research and headed straight to Google? That's one way to research. Another way is to do *action research*—where you still use technology, but you also get to do much more. As you investigate the water situation in your community and the larger world, consider using these four action research methods:

- **Media:** includes books (such as the one you are reading right now), newspapers, magazines, movies, television, and the Internet—Web pages, blogs, Facebook, YouTube, and other online sites. Think of ways you can work with different media to learn more about water related topics.

- Interview: typically involves a person with expertise or experience in a given area. You will find many experts giving advice on the pages of this book. Can you think of someone you know personally whose work involves water? You might also ask around at school or in your community or search the Web to find a good person to talk to.

- Survey: gathers information from a group of people. You read about students conducting a survey of water usage in their school and homes on page 11. Surveys help you obtain facts, opinions, and ideas. Who could you survey about water issues in your community—students, family members, neighbors, business people, government officials, scientists, or teachers? How many surveys would you want to complete to get a full perspective on the issues?

- Observation and Experience: draws upon what you already know, have seen, and have done, and what you may venture out to see starting this very moment. Have a camera? Taking photos or videos of what you see around you tells a powerful story.

As you use these research methods, note which you like best. You may find you are a budding journalist who enjoys combining interviews and photos, or a statistics wizard who loves compiling survey results. Keep these methods in mind whenever any kind of "research" is calling you.

## Be a Critical Consumer

As you investigate and research the issues and facts surrounding oceans and waterways, be aware that not everything you read or hear is accurate. It is up to you to try to separate the fact from the fiction. Consider your sources of information: are they dependable? Are they nonbiased (providing information regardless of their own interests)? Currently many diverse opinions exist about the condition of our environment, the causes of its condition, and what should be done as a result. For example, the majority of scientific opinion supports the theory that human industry plays a key role in global warming and climate change, which is potentially devastating for our planet, and yet the theory still has its detractors. Always validate your sources of information and be prepared to use this information to defend your statements and actions if needed.

# You're All Wet!

A quick look at human anatomy lets us know that going water-less is not an option. We are simply *all wet*. Our brains alone are nearly three-quarters water, our lungs are a full 90 percent water, and our bodies on average consist of 70 percent water . . . just like this water planet we live on.

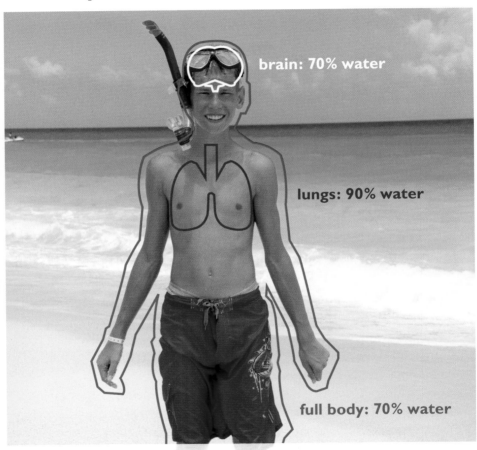

brain: 70% water

lungs: 90% water

full body: 70% water

## Life Takes Water

In addition to your body, everything about you requires water—your home is built from materials grown or produced with water. The food you eat needs water to be grown, processed, and shipped. The clothes you wear—you guessed it: water. Is there anything you use that doesn't rely on water to be produced? Not much. Check out the following chart that shows how much water is used to make, process, and transport some common goods.

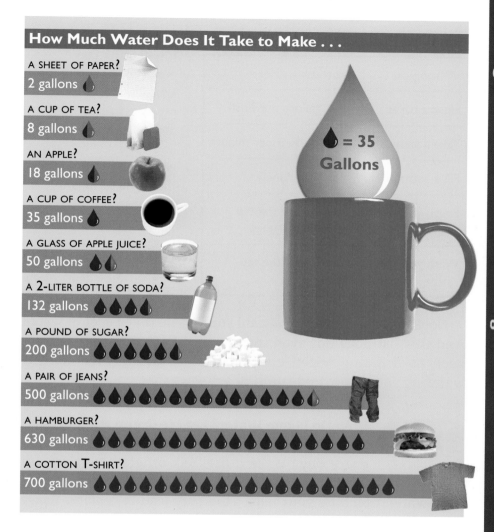

## How Much Water Does It Take to Make . . .

A SHEET OF PAPER?
2 gallons

A CUP OF TEA?
8 gallons

AN APPLE?
18 gallons

A CUP OF COFFEE?
35 gallons

A GLASS OF APPLE JUICE?
50 gallons

A 2-LITER BOTTLE OF SODA?
132 gallons

A POUND OF SUGAR?
200 gallons

A PAIR OF JEANS?
500 gallons

A HAMBURGER?
630 gallons

A COTTON T-SHIRT?
700 gallons

= 35 Gallons

Now you're probably wondering: *Why so much water?* Consider all that goes into producing these items. To make a hamburger, most of the 630 gallons of water go into growing grain to feed the cattle. To make your favorite pair of jeans, water is used to grow, process, and dye the cotton, and to keep the factory operating. Water also is used in the plant that manufactures the plastic bottle that holds your soda . . . and in the freighter that transports your Colombian-grown coffee beans to your grocery store.

What does this mean about the choices you make every day? Do your choices matter?

If you are a typical person living in the United States, you use an average of 80 to 100 gallons of water every day.

## Consider that . . .

| When you . . . | you use . . . |
|---|---|
| Flush a toilet | 5–7 gallons per flush |
| Take a shower | 7–10 gallons per minute |
| Fill a bathtub | 36–50 gallons |
| Brush your teeth | 10 gallons if the tap is running |
| Wash your hands | 2 gallons if the tap is running |

**World Water Monitoring Day** is an international education and outreach program that builds public awareness and involvement in protecting water resources around the world by engaging citizens to conduct basic monitoring of their local waterways. Visit www.worldwatermonitoringday.org for more information.

Note that even how you *discard* your waste takes a lot of water. And this list does not even include countless other activities—such as drinking water, cooking food, washing your clothes, watering your lawn, and running a dishwasher.

**YOUR TURN**

**How Do I Love Water? Let Me Count the Ways . . .** Can you think of other ways that you use water every day? Make a list. Ask others how they use water. Challenge a friend to a see who can list the most uses for water. Combine your lists. This may lead to a water usage awareness campaign in your school or community.

# TEENS IN ACTION

## Victoria, British Columbia, Canada
### Don't Be a Drip

At South Park Family School in Victoria, British Columbia, students participating in the Roots & Shoots program (see the Roots & Shoots box on page 27) decided to conserve water at school, home, and workplaces, and to teach the community how to conserve, too. They performed skits, made posters, and placed stickers at every sink, fountain, and shower in the school with the slogan: Don't be a drip—Turn me off quick!

## Colombo, Sri Lanka
### Camp Biodiversity

In Colombo, Sri Lanka, students organized a two-day camp for kids to study biodiversity in a local forest. They implemented 400 water monitoring tests using kits received from the World Water Monitoring program and constructed 20 household rainwater-saving units as models for the community to follow. When the students found five disappearing species of mango trees, they reintroduced them by cultivating 1,000 seedlings to be replanted. Along the way, they learned about the water shortages facing their communities and the importance of water conservation. Ultimately, they developed a newfound respect for environmental preservation efforts and their surrounding ecosystem.

## Nova Scotia, Canada
### Rocks in the Pot

Ecole Saint Catherine's School Roots & Shoots program in Halifax, Nova Scotia, invited a representative from Clean Nova Scotia to their school to deliver a presentation on climate change and water conservation. After becoming informed about water issues, students aimed to reduce their consumption by installing water reservoirs in the school's 45 toilets. Students collected 500mL plastic bottles from recycling bins, filled them with water and pebbles, then put two bottles in every toilet tank, reducing each flush from 13 liters to 12.

Turning off the tap is the obvious way to use less water. But it's just as easy to do what the Halifax students did to instantly turn your toilet into a low-flow version. Simply fill a used plastic bottle with water and put the full bottle in the tank of your toilet. The number of ounces that the bottle holds is how much water you save every time you flush!

EARTH**ECHO**
INTERNATIONAL

# World Water Use

Is water usage the same everywhere in the world? Not at all. People living in the United States consume the most. The following chart shows the average daily water use in some of the world's nations.

Only a small percentage of the world's population consumes the majority of its water resources.

If everyone in the United States used just *one* less gallon of water per shower daily (that's roughly six fewer seconds in the shower) . . . *85 billion* gallons of water per year would be saved.

Why do you think this is the case? Unfortunately, with all the water on our water planet, there is not an endless supply for people everywhere to use, as you will read in the next section.

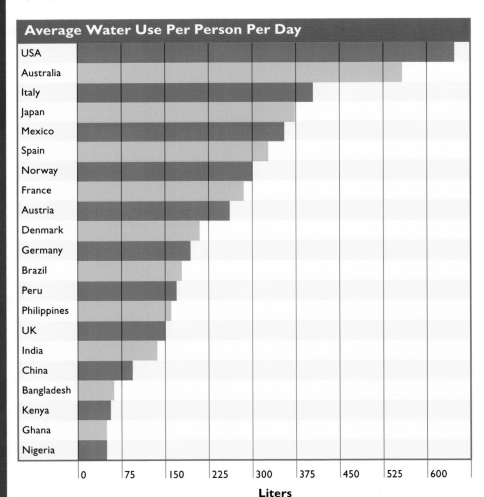

**Average Water Use Per Person Per Day**

| | | | | | | | | |
|---|---|---|---|---|---|---|---|---|
| USA | | | | | | | | |
| Australia | | | | | | | | |
| Italy | | | | | | | | |
| Japan | | | | | | | | |
| Mexico | | | | | | | | |
| Spain | | | | | | | | |
| Norway | | | | | | | | |
| France | | | | | | | | |
| Austria | | | | | | | | |
| Denmark | | | | | | | | |
| Germany | | | | | | | | |
| Brazil | | | | | | | | |
| Peru | | | | | | | | |
| Philippines | | | | | | | | |
| UK | | | | | | | | |
| India | | | | | | | | |
| China | | | | | | | | |
| Bangladesh | | | | | | | | |
| Kenya | | | | | | | | |
| Ghana | | | | | | | | |
| Nigeria | | | | | | | | |

0    75    150    225    300    375    450    525    600

**Liters**

# Water, Water Everywhere . . . or Is It?

- 71% of Earth's surface is covered by oceans.
- The average depth of the ocean is 2.5 miles.
- The average temperature of the ocean is 39 degrees Fahrenheit.
- The Pacific Ocean is the largest body of water in the world, covering 33% of Earth's surface.
- The Arctic Ocean is the smallest ocean, holding only 1% of Earth's seawater. This is still more than 25 times as much water as in all the rivers and freshwater lakes combined.
- Antarctica has as much ice as the Atlantic Ocean has water.
- The average sea level has risen between 4 and 10 inches over the past 100 years alone.
- 97% of the world's water is in the ocean.
- The largest living structure on Earth is in the ocean. It is the Great Barrier Reef, which covers an area larger than Great Britain and can be seen from space.
- Three-quarters of the world's largest cities are located by the sea.
- More than 90% of the goods traded between countries are carried by ocean freighters.

**Jane Goodall's roots&shoots**

www.rootsandshoots.org

Jane Goodall's Roots & Shoots program is a global network of young people taking action to make the world a better place. Find out more at their website.

# "How inappropriate to call this planet

## It's a Watery World

Our planet has one big connected ocean, yet there are many ocean basins, such as the Atlantic, Pacific, Indian, Arctic, and Southern. The ocean covers nearly three-quarters of Earth's surface making it mostly water, just like our bodies.

What's more, *all* water on Earth is connected—and not just on the surface. Water evaporates from the earth's surface and falls as precipitation in the form of rain, snow, and sleet back onto the land, oceans, and waterways. It then returns to the oceans as river runoff and groundwater flow. This exchange of Earth's water in the process of evaporation and precipitation is known as the *hydrologic cycle*.

Wouldn't having endless sources of new water be fantastic? Maybe these exist in fairy tales, but not in reality. Although the ocean is large, covering the vast majority of our planet, water is finite and resources are limited.

> **Today, a lot of management of natural resources isn't guided by science but by wishful thinking.**
> —Philippe Cousteau

Earth, when clearly it is planet Ocean."

—Arthur C. Clark, author

# Community Water Needs

Let's do the math: as shown on page 27, 97 percent of the world's water is ocean saltwater. Another 2 percent is locked in ice caps and glaciers. That means 99 percent of Earth's water is unfit to drink, leaving just 1 percent freshwater for consumption by all living creatures, including plants and animals.

Most likely when you want a drink of water, you turn on a tap. But can everyone in the world do this? Are we getting "tapped out" with overuse of water in some parts of the world and extremely limited water access in others? In many areas, drought has drastically reduced access to fresh water. Climate changes have resulted in parched land and low water tables. And in many locations, water supplies are contaminated or private corporations are trying to gain ownership of public water supplies, limiting people's access.

## Potable Water

Potable water is water that is drinkable—safe for human consumption. Potable water is free from pollution, harmful organisms, and impurities. In the United States, the Environmental Protection Agency (EPA), using guidelines defined by Congress in the 1974 Safe Drinking Water Act (SDWA), is responsible for setting the standards for drinking water. In addition to the EPA, each of the 50 states, plus the District of Columbia, has a governmental agency that is responsible for setting standards that meet or exceed the EPA guidelines and enforcing these drinking water standards.

## "Filthy water cannot be washed."

—West African proverb

Millions of Americans receive high-quality potable water every day from public water supply systems via their taps. However, safe drinking water cannot be taken for granted. Several things threaten public water supplies: chemicals that are improperly disposed of, animal waste, pesticides, human waste, storm water runoff, underground waste storage, and naturally occurring substances can all contaminate drinking water. Likewise, water that is not properly treated or disinfected, or that travels through a poorly maintained distribution system may also pose a health risk.

## A Thirsty World in Crisis

Internationally, the World Health Organization (WHO) is responsible for providing guidelines that can be used by all countries to define their own drinking water standards. Unfortunately, in many countries these standards are far from acceptable. It has been estimated that 1 billion people across the globe do not have access to safe drinking water. Nearly 90 percent of all diseases in the world are caused by unsafe drinking water, inadequate sanitation, and poor hygiene. Every year, 4 billion cases of diarrhea are a direct result of drinking contaminated water; this results in more than 2 million deaths each year—the equivalent of 20 passenger-filled jumbo jets crashing every day.

Boy collecting drinking water during a shortage in the capital. Delhi, India. September 2007.
© Paul Prescott | Dreamstime.com

What can be done? Potable water needs to be treated as a limited, nonrenewable resource. While the earth's hydrologic cycle shows us that water is constantly being renewed, pollution often causes the water in our air, rain, snow, and ground springs to be contaminated. It is important we take action to:

- use water more efficiently, especially in our farm irrigation methods which currently require vast amounts of water

- conserve water in our homes, schools, and businesses

- promote the reuse of water when possible

## Saving Water Worldwide

Efforts are being made around the world to save water on a daily basis. Here are a few notable ones:

- Many public facilities in the United States, Canada, and Europe have installed sinks that have motion sensors to turn water on and off, preventing water waste.

- Some facilities use special toilet attachments that flush liquid and solid waste into separate tanks enabling liquid wastewater to be filtered and reused in the toilets.

- In many U.S. cities, residents are allowed to water their lawns and gardens only on specified days and at specified times.

- In European countries and elsewhere, public showers operate on a limited time basis and shut off automatically after the allotted number of minutes.

Do the environment (and yourself!) a favor and use a dishwasher instead of doing dishes by hand. An automatic dishwasher uses an average of six fewer gallons of hot water per cycle (or over 2,000 gallons per year) than hand washing.

**EARTH ECHO**
INTERNATIONAL

**YOUR TURN**

### Get Involved with Potable Water

As kids learn about the potable water crisis across the globe, many are compelled to action. Find out what they are doing and how you can join in the cause at these sites:

**Ryan's Well Foundation** (www.ryanswell.ca) Meet Ryan Hreljac, who joined the clean water cause in 1998 at age 6; his foundation has since taken on over 500 projects in 16 countries, bringing clean water and sanitation services to over 640,000 people.

**Clean Water Action** (www.cleanwateraction.org) is a U.S. grassroots organization working to empower people to take action to protect the nation's waters, build healthy communities, and make democracy work for all of us.

**Water.org** (www.water.org) is a nonprofit organization whose founders have transformed hundreds of communities in developing nations—Africa, South Asia, and Latin America—by providing access to safe water and sanitation.

# TEENS IN ACTION

## Ayni, Tajikistan
### Teaching Clean Water

Students from a secondary school in Tajikistan planned "Alternative Approaches to Water Supply." Their home is in the Ayni district, an isolated mountainous area physically cut off from the rest of the country for four to five months a year due to heavy snow and undeveloped roads. The local economy is based on a mix of animal herding, orchard tending, and trade, and they rely on open water sources, which often carry diseases. Ayni students conducted activities with younger children, teaching them how to boil water, use chlorine tablets to keep water clean, and wash their hands, and why all of these things are necessary.

## Mumbai, India
### The Changemakers

High school students at Phillips Academy in Massachusetts traveled to Mumbai to participate in an event called *Niswarth*, which is the Hindu translation of the school's motto, "not for self." The Phillips students partnered with students from Udayachal High School in Mumbai and two local nongovernmental organizations to help in one of the city's poorest slums. The group was invited to shanties that stood next door to some of the most expensive real estate in the world. As part of an ongoing census, students went door to door in one building listening to concerns and complaints of residents, a common one being: "We get clean water in our homes for only 20 minutes every three days."

**Want to know more about potable water? Visit these sites:**

**Safe Drinking Water Act (SDWA):** www.epa.gov/safewater/sdwa

**LifeStraw:** www.vestergaard-frandsen.com/lifestraw.htm

**World Health Organization (WHO) Drinking Water:**
www.who.int/topics/drinking_water

**Centers for Disease Control (CDC) Drinking Water:**
www.cdc.gov/healthywater/drinking

**Project WET—World Water Education:** www.projectwet.org

Drawing from their studies of this and similar communities, consultations with their partners, and extensive discussions with local students, the team decided to address this dire need for clean water. Upon learning that India's newly enacted Right to Information Act mandated a timely response to citizen requests, the students drafted a petition for increased access to water. They obtained signatures from every resident of the building, and then delivered the petition to the local warden.

Consider volunteering with organizations that help our environment like the ones listed in this book. Getting involved builds skills and experience that will prove valuable in school and beyond.

While they awaited an answer to the petition, the students created a plan that could be sustained by local residents. They cleaned the filthy building using monsoon rainwater. Soon residents were joining the cleaning effort. "If you care so much about our living conditions," one woman said, "we should take similar responsibility." They even created a pulley system to bring buckets of water from the street to the top floor. When residents of the neighboring building witnessed these efforts, they tackled their own hallways with buckets of rainwater. Meanwhile, the warden responded within a week to the students' petition and informed the residents of the newly cleaned building, as well as over 25,000 neighboring residents, that their access to clean water would now be eight minutes every day—far from ideal, but a vast improvement.

Almost a year later, the hallways of the Mumbai apartment building are dirty again. Still, the effects of the students' visit remains. The building's residents are less distrustful and are addressing new issues such as the quality of local schools and access to medical facilities. A sustainable transformation seems to be taking place.

**❝ I have a burning inspiration to go out into the world, pursue my passion, and make change. I can no longer be content with simply standing on the sideline. ❞**
—*Zahra, age 16, Phillips Academy student*

### Burkina Faso, Africa
*Moringa to the Rescue!*

In the town of Niankorodougou, Burkina Faso, the Club du Science consists of the top two science students in each grade from the local junior high schools. The club studied gardening and after reviewing uses for many of the area's native trees, they chose to focus on the many benefits of moringa trees. Originally from India, *moringa oliefera* is a tree adapting remarkably well in Africa due to its low water needs and rapid growth. The leaves of the tree provide a good source of vitamin A, vitamin C, potassium, calcium, and protein. Scientists claim that moringa helps prevent over 300 illnesses.

A moringa tree in Etosha National Park, Namibia.

In addition, grains taken from the branches of the tree can be used as a water treatment. Peace Corps member Adelaide Schwartz explains: "So many of the sicknesses here are waterborne. Clean water is hard to obtain. The moringa grain acts like a flocculent, which means when it is added to a bucket of water, within a few minutes a film can be scooped from the top leaving behind clean water." With assistance from Ms. Schwartz and their teacher Mr. Some, the club members took their knowledge of moringa trees to the local health clinic and planned their course of action. They explained the benefits of the tree to clinic workers and planted ten trees for use in the surrounding community. Students continue to provide needed information through a community awareness campaign showing how moringa grains can be used to purify water. They also partnered with a science club at Hallettsville Junior High in Texas and sent them lessons and videos all the way from Burkina Faso.

Mr. Some remarked, "Months later, the kids still talk about our moringa project at the health center because they see the trees in their village and still use the seeds at home. They are proud to be able to help their families, and proud to have shared their knowledge with a U.S. classroom."

# Water Privatization

Water privatization is the process by which corporations (and sometimes governments) take control of public water supplies for private sale. Water is a $400 billion industry—the third largest in the world, behind electricity and oil. This includes private corporations that sell bottled water, as well as those that pump, disinfect, transport, and control access to water.

## Water Is Big Business

Bottled water costs thousands of times more than tap water to produce.

The United States produces 40 billion plastic bottles each year, which requires about 17.6 million barrels of oil—enough to fuel about 1.5 million cars a year.

Most Americans pay $0.002 per gallon for unfiltered tap water. Filtering tap water with a counter top unit costs $0.25 per gallon, and filtering it with a unit under the sink only costs about $0.10 per gallon.

Bottled water typically costs about $1 for an 8- to 12-ounce bottle, amounting to more than $10 per gallon.

In the United States, water privatization is typically the result of corporations using public water supplies and private wells to produce bottled water. Overseas, especially in underdeveloped countries, privatization often involves both the production of bottled water and the entire water infrastructure—the means to pump, distribute, and sell the water.

How much water can safely be privatized? A typical water bottling plant might take anywhere from 100 million to 300 million gallons a year from a public water supply. This heavy use of public water systems can threaten local water table levels, groundwater flow rates, and conditions of local bodies of water.

Also, if some people have free access to natural resources and others do not, could this cause conflicts? Absolutely. Global conflict between countries is increasingly likely to stem from the lack of available natural resources (food, water, oil, farmland) and the political and economic consequences of this lack of necessities. Already, water disputes are brewing among 50 countries on five continents that share freshwater reserves. Sensitive negotiations must occur quickly to determine how these nations will share rivers, reservoirs, and groundwater.

Women collecting water from a public pipe during a water rationing period. Bhaktapur, Nepal. December 2009.

© Shariff Che' Lah | Dreamstime.com

## time for
## REFLECTION

"Hey, that water is mine!" What do you think of people owning what previously has been public water? Should we privatize our natural resources and pay for their use? Consider the pros and cons. Who might benefit? Who might lose out?

# Bottled Water

People in the United States buy an estimated 34.6 billion single-serving bottles of water a year—up from 3.3 billion in 1997. Worldwide, 2.7 million tons of plastic are used each year to make water bottles, and in the United States, less than 20 percent of these plastic bottles are recycled. Does using all this plastic and drinking the water inside make a difference?

In most cases, tap water actually follows higher purity standards than bottled water.

In 2006, more than 17 million barrels of oil was used to manufacture plastic water bottles and generated more than 2.5 million tons of carbon dioxide.

While some are recycled, a whopping 9 out of 10 water bottles like this one end up as garbage or litter, which equals 30 million bottles. U.S. cities pay around $70 million every year in costs related to trash cleanup and landfills.

The process of manufacturing a plastic water bottle requires three times the amount of water that is needed to fill it.

About 40% of bottled water originated as tap water.

It could take over 1,000 years for this plastic bottle to biodegrade (naturally decompose).

This bottle contains chemicals called plasticizers, or *phthalates* (pronounced THAL-ates). These seep into the water over time, posing health risks such as hormone disruption and cancer.

In summary, the environmental impacts of plastic-bottled water are impossible to ignore any longer. They include:

- huge oil resources are used to create the bottles

- water resources are depleted in local communities where water is harvested

- health risks are associated with water that isn't as strictly regulated as tap water

- toxic chemicals such as phthalates seep into the water from the plastic

- a large volume of waste is generated and usually not recycled

## How Can the Plastic Water Bottle Problem Be Solved?

1. "What if I just reuse one plastic bottle for a while before buying a new one?"

   Not so fast. Reusing plastic bottles often means that more and more phthalates are released into the liquid inside. As previously noted, phthalates have been shown to cause cancer and disrupt bodily hormones. In addition, plastic bottles can harbor harmful bacterial growth inside any cracks or crevices that may form over time.

Plastic bottles and other waste floating on a lake.

2. "What about buying in bulk—2 liters at a time instead of 12 ounces?"

This can help reduce the waste, although it doesn't eliminate the oil and water depletion issues or the health concerns.

3. "Let's recycle all the bottles!"

Again, this is necessary to help reduce waste, but it still won't address other concerns. Also, recycling water bottles requires a lot of energy resources and—you guessed it—water.

4. "Let's make the water bottle companies adhere to stricter water quality standards."

This could help decrease the health risks from the water, but not from the phthalates in the plastic bottle. Also, it could lead to higher production costs, which could make the bottles of water even more expensive.

5. "How about just . . . not buying so much bottled water?"

At the core of the water bottle issue is a simple case of supply and demand. If consumers (like you and me) cut back on the purchasing of plastic water bottles—instead drinking water from nonplastic containers—what might happen to the supply? It will sit in warehouses, unsold, which means companies will likely stop manufacturing so many bottles.

So what *are* people in the real world—teens in particular—doing about this issue?

Remember that soda, sports drinks, and juices are also bottled "water." Instead of using a disposable plastic bottle, invest in a reusable stainless steel one. If you do buy a plastic bottle, always recycle it, or use it as a water-saving device in your toilet (see page 25).

EARTH**ECHO**
INTERNATIONAL

# TEENS IN ACTION

## Chagrin Falls, Ohio, United States
### Go Green—Drink Tap

In Chagrin Falls, Ohio, the youth board of Community Partnerships for Youth created an awareness campaign about the destructive nature of disposable water bottles culminating in a Go Green Water Tasting. Stationed in a shopping center, the kids invited passersby to taste two water samples, choose the one they liked best, and then guess which sample was bottled water and which came from the tap. The tasters overall preferred tap water and guessed incorrectly that it was bottled water. Students gave out *Go Green—Drink Tap* T-shirts, bumper stickers, and non-disposable water bottles. Sharing facts in the community and in school raised awareness that not only is tap water better for the environment, it also tastes better than bottled water.

## Okanogan, Washington, United States
### GEAR UP for Recycling

What do you do if your school sells drinks in plastic bottles but doesn't offer a way to recycle the empties? You GEAR UP for recycling. The GEAR UP program was planned, budgeted, implemented, and presented by sophomores at Okanogan High School in Washington. They set out to educate students, parents, and community members on the importance of recycling plastic bottles and the harmful effects on the environment when recycling does not take place. By educating the community and city council, they hope to spearhead an ongoing plastic bottle recycling program in their school and community.

### YOUR TURN
### A Reusable Bottle Campaign

Do we need plastic water bottles or is there a better idea, like using stainless steel, aluminum, canvas, or some other type of material? Brainstorm the best alternatives and come up with ways to convince people that we are better off avoiding plastic bottles. Then, design a logo, think of a slogan, create posters, start a blog, alert the media, post a video—and make your community a plastic-bottle-free zone!

# Where's the Water in Your Backyard?

Think of your own backyard—your community. Can you see the water flowing or rippling in a river, a creek, a pond, a lake, or an ocean? Or is it invisible, churning underground, resting in a marsh, or swirling in a hidden reservoir? Water is continually on the move, all around you. What's the connection between all the different ways that water travels? **Watersheds.** The entire planet is a watershed in which all the water eventually ends up in the ocean. But within this giant watershed are thousands of smaller ones, all working together.

A **watershed** is an area of land where all of the water that is under it or drains off of it flows into the same place.

Watersheds are everywhere and come in many sizes and diverse shapes. They flow between city, state, and national boundaries. In the United States and Puerto Rico, there are 2,267 watersheds.

Knowing about your watershed matters. This helps you take care of your corner of the ecosystem.

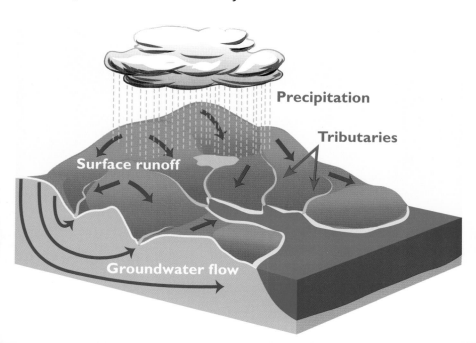

Precipitation

Tributaries

Surface runoff

Groundwater flow

Watersheds are very busy places. They create diverse habitats for all kinds of animals—both large and microscopic. They react to various weather conditions, cope with soil erosion, and deal with the impacts of choices made by humans every day. Any new construction project changes a watershed and may disrupt a home of beavers or prevent tadpoles from becoming frogs. Paving over a pond with cement for a parking lot can cause confusion for migrating animals. How we develop and live in our communities can create a disturbance.

In addition to these more localized watersheds, 114 major land watersheds of the world cover multiple countries and parts of entire continents.

And to make matters even more exciting, our planet can be divided according to *ocean* watersheds.

But however you divide up the planet, the most important fact is: the watersheds that you depend on for all your daily water needs also depend on *you*—to preserve the habitats, to keep the areas clean and free of pollution, to allow animals to thrive, and to enjoy the beauty of our natural world.

### YOUR TURN

### Know Your Watershed

Do some action research. What does your local watershed look like? What waterways are closest to you? Find out—and add more to the list!

- Creek
- Lake
- Pond
- Ocean
- Sea
- River
- Canal
- Aquifer (groundwater well or spring)
- Estuary (bay, lagoon, or river mouth)
- Salt marsh (seawater swamp)
- Stream
- Wetland (freshwater swamp)
- Other?

Begin to look for clues about how your waters are interconnected. How? Get out there and explore. Find the waterway closest to your home, school, or community center, and follow along its perimeter to examine how it connects to other water sources. You might be surprised about what you find. Then, create a diagram that shows this interconnectivity—be inventive! Mix photos and art. Insert a picture of what you found along the water's edge. Use this to inform others and inspire them to learn more. Visit www.epa.gov/adopt to participate in EPA's Adopt Your Watershed program in your area.

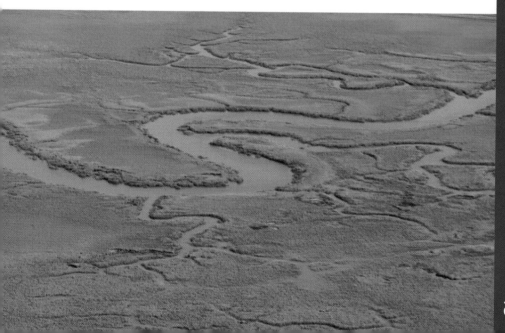

# Your Piece of the Watershed

Let's examine watersheds more closely by looking at different parts of this ecological puzzle. Along the way, be thinking of ways you can investigate a community need and take action.

## Rivers and Creeks

Rivers and creeks are made of fresh water usually beginning on a hill or mountain. The headwater, or river source at its highest elevation, might be a single small stream. However, as the river flows downstream, more water gathers from springs, rain, runoff, other rivers and streams, and basically any water that happens to come along for the ride. Can you imagine all the uses that rivers serve? From crop irrigation to transportation, recreation, food, and energy, rivers keep industry going, crops growing, and people moving.

In North America, the largest watershed is the Mississippi River basin. Every continent has rivers except for one. Can you guess which one? (See answer at the bottom of this page.)

### The World's Most Endangered Rivers

Endangered rivers are not always the most polluted; they may also be rivers that developers and industries are in the process of making important decisions about. The term "endangered" means that if the right decisions are not made, these rivers may be damaged and made unfit for wildlife to live in them, for animals and humans to drink, or for crop irrigation. Some decisions may even change the way the whole watershed operates, or lead to the elimination of the river altogether. As shown in the following charts, these decisions typically involve water removal, dams, overdevelopment, pollution, industry, or climate change.

Remember, water equals *life*. These rivers are at risk, which means the people around them are at risk of losing their livelihoods as well as their daily water supply. Animal life is at risk, too. In the past few decades alone, over 20 percent of the planet's 10,000 freshwater fish species have become extinct or endangered.

*Answer: Antarctica.*

## The Top 10 Endangered Rivers in the United States

| River | Location | Primary Threat |
|---|---|---|
| Sacramento-San Joaquin River System | California | Poor flood management |
| Flint River | Georgia | Low water supply |
| Lower Snake River | Washington, Oregon, Idaho | Too many dams |
| Mattawoman Creek | Maryland | Urban development |
| North Fork of the Flathead River | Montana | Coal mining |
| Saluda River | South Carolina | Sewage pollution |
| Laurel Hill Creek | Pennsylvania | Water over-extraction |
| Beaver Creek | Arkansas | Oil and gas development |
| Pascagula River | Mississippi | Petroleum storage |
| Lower St. Croix National Scenic Riverway | Minnesota, Wisconsin | Poor industrial zoning |

## The Top 10 Endangered Rivers in the World

| River | Location | Primary Threat |
|---|---|---|
| Salween | Southeast Asia | Too many dams |
| Danube | Europe | Poor navigation infrastructure |
| La Plata | South America | Too many dams and poor navigation infrastructure |
| Rio Grande—Rio Bravo | Southern United States and Mexico | Water over-extraction |
| Ganges | South and Central Asia | Water over-extraction |
| Indus | South and Central Asia | Climate change |
| Nile—Lake Victoria | Africa | Climate change |
| Murray—Darling | Australia | Invasive species |
| Mekong | Southeast Asia | Overfishing |
| Yangtze | China | Pollution |

# TEENS IN ACTION

## Mooresville, Indiana, United States
### Cleaning the White River

Imagine a news article with this headline: *Dogs Dying from Drinking the Local River Water.* When students in Mooresville, Indiana, read this headline about the river running through their town, they decided to tackle the issue. With support from their teacher, the students took action through the **Project Citizen program.**

What did the students of Mooresville do? Two of them, Luke and Stevie, tell us . . .

*Project Citizen* is a national education program that helps students advocate for policy change in their local government. Students identify a problem in their community, come up with a solution, and implement an action plan.

For more information, visit www.civiced.com.

**"** The first step we took was to become certified water quality testers through Indiana's Department of Natural Resources. Our teacher took a seven-hour course, so we could receive the materials to begin our work. After months of water testing, interviews with scientists, and research, we realized that the water *wasn't* actually dirty enough to kill a dog. However, we still had two major problems with our local White River: erosion causing floods, and failing septic tanks causing high levels of nitrogen and E coli in the water, high enough to kill aquatic life.

### Learning on the River

The Earth Conservation Corps is located on the heavily polluted Anacostia River in Southeast Washington, D.C., one the nation's most disadvantaged communities. ECC provides unemployed, out-of-school young people ages 17–25 with hands-on workforce training and environmental education, while the young people help restore and clean the Anacostia River and surrounding communities. Find out more at www.ecc1.org.

"Our solution to erosion was to buffer the riverbanks with trees. We planted 100 trees in the local area, and we hope to plant more. In addition, we proposed a tax-rebate for those citizens who cleaned their septic tank, and our mayor approved it.

"Our efforts are well connected to what we do in our classes, especially in mathematics, science, language arts, and social studies. We begin with water testing—a combination of computation and measurement skills. On the science side, we learned that the numbers are based on such variables as fertilizers, pesticides, increased photosynthesis, and nitrogen. For language arts, we have written three grant applications raising over $5,000 for equipment and tree planting. Our team has published an article in our newspaper. We read endlessly about water quality during our research, and mastered our public speaking skills by presenting to the governor, mayor, city council, school board, and state department of natural resources.

Our voice matters. We have brought real change and solved community problems . . . and our work goes on! 🙚

—*Luke Clair-Ficko and Stevie Hoffman,*
*Mooresville High School students*

# Estuaries

An estuary is a semi-enclosed coastal body of water connected to the open sea that includes a mix of freshwater and seawater. Common estuaries include bays, harbors, inlets, lagoons, river mouths, and wetlands. Throughout history, we have depended on estuaries for trade, food, and shelter from the unpredictable open ocean water. Two major U.S. estuaries, the Chesapeake Bay and San Francisco Bay, are home to large economically and militarily important harbors where many ships pass each year.

Estuaries are home to a large variety of plants and animals that we depend on for food. Huge numbers of commercially valuable fish from the ocean seek out estuaries to spawn in the protected waters. Oysters, clams, and other shellfish thrive in bays and inlets, as do many species of crabs.

Any trash or sediment in a river naturally ends up in an estuary, since the current of the river slows here due to widening or merging with the ocean's tide. This pollution can have long-term impacts on the health of an estuary. Chemical contaminates can linger in bottom sediments for years, which has caused many areas to be closed for fishing until the chemical has broken down. Excessive loads of silt and other sediments caused by erosion can suffocate bottom-dwelling plants and animals. In addition, disruption of the flow of a river due to damming and irrigation can cause salty water to progress upstream and threaten freshwater species.

Development is another danger estuaries face. Rising human populations are looking for places to expand, and what was once considered marginal land is sometimes now economically valuable. Wetlands are being filled in and mangrove swamps destroyed for housing and industrial purposes—an estimated 215 million acres of the world's estuaries have been lost this way. Not only do we lose primary habitat for many animals and plants, but we also lose an important buffer zone. Wetlands are remarkably good at using plants and microbes to break down chemical compounds and metals from runoff pollution. They also help trap carbon and are important in the fight against climate change. Finally, estuaries often act as crucial storm barriers in places such as the Louisiana bayou.

### Shelter from the Storm

For years prior to Hurricane Katrina in 2003, oil and gas companies and private developers had been tunneling through and paving over the wetlands that separated New Orleans and surrounding communities from the Gulf of Mexico. Without this natural shelter zone fully in tact, the devastation caused by Katrina was far worse in these cities than it might otherwise have been.

Visit www.epa.gov/wetlands for more information about how you can get involved in restoring crucial wetlands.

# TEENS IN ACTION

## Alameda, California, United States

### Save the Bay

The San Francisco Bay is the largest estuary on the west coast of the Americas and serves many important natural functions. The bay also faces numerous challenges—from pollution to overdevelopment. Area students are involved in a wide range of projects investigating the bay and local creeks, while examining the human practices that can harm or help the bay. What's being done?

In honor of Earth Day, science students at Wood Middle School in Alameda, California, took their concerns to the beach. They learned about the process of **bioaccumulation**, in which small sea creatures mistake microscopic bits of plastic for food and are poisoned when they ingest it. The students cleaned up a quarter-mile long segment of beach next to their school, removing and cataloguing all types of trash.

The students identified litter from Halloween candy wrappers as potential debris that could enter the San Francisco Bay ecosystem and cause harm. So in the fall, they wrote letters to the editors of local newspapers, advocating for children to properly dispose of litter.

**Bioaccumulation** is the gradual buildup of a chemical in a living organism. This happens because 1) the chemical piles up faster than it can be metabolized, or 2) the chemical simply can't be metabolized. If this chemical is toxic to the organism, then the buildup becomes a health concern. Common toxic chemicals come from plastics, pesticides used on farm crops, car emissions, and mercury from coal-burning and other industries.

**Save the Bay** helps Wood Middle School and many other schools to protect our oceans and waterways. Visit www.savesfbay.org.

49

" Every year around Halloween I realize that children throw plastic candy wrappers on the ground. These piles of nondegradable plastic go into the drains and right into the ocean. The fish in the sea think the plastic is food. And the seagulls—who eat *anything*—eat the wrappers and the fish. The plastic wrapper blocks the throat and the stomach and kills these animals! If we could just remind parents and children not to litter, there would be less work for the environment and for the trash collectors. Please help. The world lies in our hands. "

—Lhadze Bosiljevac, grade 8

# Lakes

Oh, go jump in the lake! But wait . . . is the lake clean? Have pollutants been building over time from boating or shipping traffic or industrial waste? Does the lake even have water in it? By definition, a lake is a body of (usually) freshwater surrounded by land. It is larger than a pond, has a river that feeds it, and is not directly a part of the ocean. However, a lake can also be a dry basin waiting for water to seasonally fill it in.

## Do You Know Your Lake Facts?
*(See answers at the bottom of this page.)*

1. Which country has more than 60% of the world's lakes?

2. Which country is known as "The Land of the Thousand Lakes"?

3. Which of the 50 United States is known as "The Land of Ten Thousand Lakes"?

4. Which Canadian province boasts 100,000 lakes?

Canada, Finland, Minnesota, Manitoba

What creates a lake? Landslides, glaciers, sinkholes, a slow moving river bend, or a volcanic crater that fills with precipitation—these are just a few origins of lakes. We humans have made our share of lakes by building dams or diverting water sources for irrigation or drinking water reservoirs. Once in existence, lakes continually change through erosion, climate changes, and human use.

Think of a lake you live by or that you care about. This lake, like all lakes, needs to be clean and safe for the animals and plants that inhabit its water and the surrounding area. Sadly this is not always the case. Recreation, agriculture, mining, and other activities can disrupt the health of these crucial water systems.

## Lake Superior Beaches Closed Due to Contamination

In recent years, Lake Superior beaches in Duluth, Minnesota, frequently have been closed in summer due to high amounts of bacteria, including *E coli*, in the water. The primary sources of the bacteria appear to be nearby wastewater treatment plants and feces contamination of migrating water birds such as terns, geese, and gulls. This is just one example of a growing trend of U.S. beach closings—in both lakes and coastal areas—due to pollution. In a 2009 report, the total number of beach closing days topped 20,000 for the fourth year in a row.

Before visiting a beach near you, investigate its water quality here: www.nrdc.org/water/oceans and click on "Testing the Waters." Or, visit www.surfrider.org/stateofthebeach.

A beach is closed due to chemical pollution of the water.

# TEENS IN ACTION

## Chicago, Illinois, United States
### Calumet Is My Backyard

The Lake Calumet region of Chicago is situated in the Lake Michigan watershed. During the early 20th century, Lake Calumet was home to major industrial development. Since that time, most of the steel mills have closed, leaving degraded natural areas behind especially susceptible to invasive species (often called "weeds") like dogwood, buckthorn, and garlic mustard. That's where CIMBY comes in, which stands for "Calumet Is My Backyard," a partnership between schools and local organizations. CIMBY connects high school environmental science students with opportunities to be stewards in the Lake Calumet area of Chicago's southeast side. Throughout the year students adopt one of Calumet's natural sites—wetlands, prairies, forest preserves, savannah woodlands, marshes—and put their learning to use. For the past ten years, students have built trails, solved erosion problems, gathered seeds for planting, tested and monitored water quality, examined biodiversity factors, and provided general stewardship to support their adopted site. As for the invasive species, students work together to remove these plants and reintroduce native species to the area. They are saving their neighborhood's entire ecosystem!

## Lake Chilika, India
### Clean It Up and Talk It Up

Lake Chilika in India is the largest body of brackish water (a mix of salt water and freshwater) in Asia. As part of Global Youth Service Day, 120 students from a local school joined to clean the lake and spread the word of the harmful impact of tourism. By creating and distributing multilingual pamphlets and starting information campaigns, the kids were able to reach over 1,200 local residents and visitors.

## YOUR TURN

**Turning Back Time**
In your region, what event in history left a problem to be solved? Research an industry that may have had a local impact and what was done to remedy the situation. How has your community responded to ecological problems in the past? And, most importantly, what can you do now? Local libraries, historical societies, and environmental groups can provide information, guidance, and may already have action plans in place that you can join.

**Global Youth Service Day (GYSD)**
Established in 1988, GYSD occurs in over 100 countries each year and is the largest service event in the world. On GYSD, children and teens address the world's most critical issues by partnering with families, schools, community, organizations, businesses, and governments.
Visit www.ysa .org/gysd.

## Coastal Areas

What do you like to do at the ocean shore? Surf, sunbathe, build giant sandcastles, picnic, swim, fish, sail, kayak, hike, camp? Beaches offer us adventure, play, and relaxation. While you may be out bodysurfing, others are working to make this possible. In fact, entire cities, regions, and countries depend on the money tourists spend while visiting their ocean shores.

Erosion, the wearing away of rock and soil, is a major creative force of many beaches. Erosion provides sand for new beaches and the maintenance of old ones. Erosion forms the stacks and arches found along rocky coastlines, and it provides the material that forms deltas and barrier islands. A certain amount of erosion is natural and necessary. But what happens when people try to control these shifting sands and build permanent structures, such as houses, restaurants, shops, and hotels, close to the shore? Then, erosion becomes a problem. Beaches can naturally disappear over time, or even overnight during severe storms.

"We cannot say we love the land and then take steps to destroy it for use by future generations."
—Pope John Paul II (Karol Wojtyla)

Of all the types of pollution that beaches endure, oil spills are perhaps the most deadly. A layer of thick oil quickly smothers most small animals, and larger animals that get away are poisoned soon after. Beaches do recover over time, but decades may pass before new communities of plants and animals migrate back to an affected area.

A dead oiled guillemot found during the Erika oil spill in France, 1999.

Photo credit: Sascha Regmann/Project Blue Sea/Marine Photobank

❝The oil that gets dispersed into the water will have consequences and impacts on this area for decades to come. Anyone who thinks otherwise is just not paying attention. There's still oil from the Exxon Valdez oil spill 20 years ago in Prince William Sound. These things don't go away.❞
—Philippe Cousteau, speaking about the BP oil spill in the Gulf of Mexico in April 2010

Other kinds of pollution take their toll on beaches as well. Garbage that washes up on shore can strangle, entrap, or poison wildlife. Sea turtles, for example, often mistake plastic bags for jellyfish, and many have died as a result of eating the bags. Industrial waste is often fatal to many kinds of sea life, as well. Raw sewage has caused dangerous algal blooms (toxic algae colonies), and, along with excessive fertilizer runoff, contributes to the formation of deadly "red tides," where the water is colored red by huge numbers of poisonous algal blooms. These algal blooms have been partly responsible for an increase in "dead zones," or coastal areas that once supported abundant marine life but have grown so oxygen-depleted they are now lifeless. A 2008 study counted 405 dead zones worldwide, the largest covering over 27,000 square miles.

# TEENS IN ACTION

## Honolulu, Hawai'i, United States
### Preserving Ka'ena Point

Jutting out from the westernmost tip of O'ahu, Ka'ena Point is a sacred site. Early Hawai'ians revered the rugged and remote area as a place where departing spirits leapt into the ancestral realm. Today, Ka'ena Point is a 59-acre state-owned nature reserve and remains one of Hawai'i's last coastal ecosystems, harboring nesting seabirds, monk seals, and native plants. However, after decades of overuse by visitors and rutting by four-wheel-drive vehicles, the sand dunes of Ka'ena Point are rapidly eroding into the sea.

Eighth graders at Punahou School in Honolulu have become part of a community effort to preserve and restore this endangered coastline. Teams started off by planting seedlings of native plants along a scarred section of the dunes. They hope the plants will halt the erosion and restore the pristine natural habitat.

Photo credit: Dario Salgado

"We felt if we could plant seeds, both literally and metaphorically, the kids could go back year after year and see the fruit of their labor."

—Dave Blanchette, Punahou School teacher

Ka'ena Point, Hawai'i

For many students, this was their first visit to Ka'ena Point. "It was such a remote place; everything looked perfect and it was just us and a couple of people fishing," marveled Chasen, age 14. "We had to be peaceful and mindful of this place." After offering a traditional Hawai'ian chant, the students went to work constructing a protective sand barrier, planting the seeds along eroded gullies, and posting signs to prohibit vehicles. The students collectively planted 200 seedlings. "We had a lot of teamwork," said Jackie, age 14, describing the coordinated effort to lug gallons of water, mulch, and plants across the dry landscape. Chasen agreed that the physical challenge of the half-day hike brought the students closer together.

"It feels good to give back to the environment. When people come back in later years, they will see a better place and it's good to know that we helped make it better."—Chasen, age 14

## Summary

**Investigation.** By investigating, you've learned the facts, read the stories, and heard the results. Investigation helps clarify what is going on around you—especially the underlying issues, the history, and the causes. At the same time, doing investigation introduces you to possible service partners, raises your own awareness, and shows where action is needed. Perhaps most of all, it helps you discover your own unique skills and talents that you will bring into the world of doing service.

Photo credit: David Makepeace

# STAGE 2
## DIVE IN→PREPARE

You have investigated and chosen the community water need you want to address. Now it's time to move on to the second stage of your service learning journey: preparing yourself for action by gaining an in-depth understanding of the larger water system you aim to help.

# The Story of Tar Creek: Part #2
## Miami, Oklahoma, United States
*(continued from page 18)*

## How Did They Prepare?

Through regular classes like science and English and extracurricular work, students conducted extensive research on a range of topics including water contamination and the results of human exposure to toxic heavy metals, namely lead. They learned about the causes and effects of **lead poisoning** in humans and animals. They tested Tar Creek waters. They asked experts at major universities and in government and tribal councils for more information about repairing the land and protecting the community. They wanted to find out if fish would ever swim in Tar Creek again.

### Lead Poisoning

- Human exposure to high levels of lead is extremely toxic and can be fatal.

- People can get lead in their bodies by breathing or swallowing lead dust.

- Lead exposure can harm young children and babies even before they are born.

- Even children who seem healthy can have high levels of lead in their bodies.

The Story of Tar Creek continues on page 102.

**Tar Creek sampling.** Photo credit: University of Oklahoma School of Civil Engineering and Environmental Science

# The Amazing Ocean

To fully understand the issues faced in the planet's waterways—from Miami, Oklahoma, to Cairo, Egypt, to Sydney, Australia—you first need to understand what's happening at the hub of all these waterways: the ocean.

If you think of the planet's streams, creeks, lakes, and rivers as the veins in our bodies, the ocean is our heart where all the waters meet. With the following facts, stories, and words of wisdom from people who care deeply about this watery heart, you will be poised to dive in. Are you ready? Take a deep breath . . .

The ocean supplies over half of Earth's oxygen.

The Earth has one big connected ocean with many ocean basins, such as the Atlantic, Pacific, Indian, Arctic, and Southern.

97% of Earth's water is in the ocean.

Ocean life ranges in size from the smallest living organism, a virus, to the largest animal that has ever lived on Earth, the blue whale.

The ocean provides food, medicines, minerals, energy resources, jobs, and transportation of goods and people, and plays a role in many countries' national security.

Nearly half of the world's population lives in coastal areas.

The ocean covers about 70% of the planet's surface.

"Every time you step off the land into the liquid—into the ocean—you're traveling somewhere very few people venture. You've immediately embarked on a great adventure."—*Tierney Thys, marine biologist*

# The Carbon Conundrum:
## Part #1—Ocean Acidification

The three main threats to the health of our oceans today are ocean acidification, climate change, and pollution. Of these three, two are caused by a common enemy: carbon, which exists in water and air primarily as the gas carbon dioxide, or $CO_2$.

Climate change, a.k.a. global warming, is, of course, very hot news. You've heard by now how burning fossil fuels threatens our environment by trapping heat in the atmosphere, creating "greenhouse gases." The worst offender of these gases is $CO_2$, created mainly by burning coal and oil into the air from factories, cars, and farms. But what you might not know is that $CO_2$ can also damage our oceans by causing ocean acidification (OA). Increasing $CO_2$ levels in our environment changes the ocean's chemistry. As the ocean is forced to absorb increasing amounts of carbon, the ocean's **pH level** decreases and the water becomes more and more acidic.

The ocean has absorbed about a third of the carbon that we've spewed into the atmosphere since the Industrial Revolution began nearly 200 years ago. For a while many people thought this was a good thing—better in the oceans than in the air, right? *Wrong.* Scientists later realized that when the ocean becomes acidic, calcium extraction from the water becomes difficult for sea creatures that depend on this calcium to build their shells, like coral, crabs, oysters, and lobsters. What happens if they are left without the defenses of their shells? They die, and the bottom of the food chain is disrupted. That's bad news for all of us.

**pH Level**

Water everywhere carries nutrients, oxygen, and biochemicals from place to place. The amount of acid in water can be measured by a scale called pH, which stands for "potential hydrogen." A low pH number indicates high acidity, while a high pH number means low acidity. The pH scale runs from 0 to 14, with 7 being neutral. Ocean water typically has a pH level of around 8, which means it's a base, not an acid, although it is growing more acidic.

# Food Chain, Interrupted

Increased carbon pollution causes a rise in our ocean's acid levels, which affects the overall health of the ocean . . . and may disrupt the entire planet's dinner, a.k.a. the food chain. Earth's food chain is made up of all its living organisms—from bacteria to plants to fish to pigs to humans—that depend on each other as food sources to survive.

A summary of how carbon pollution affects the food chain:

- Ocean water absorbs the CO2 released into the air when we burn fossil fuels.

- This causes the pH in the water to decrease, making the water more acidic.

- The acidic water affects small sea creatures by weakening their protective shells, which leads to their deaths.

- When the smaller creatures die, less food is available for the larger fish to eat, so they die, too.

- All of this equals less fish for bears, humans, and other mammals to eat.

Here are some specific examples:

The tiny mollusk *Limacina helicina* (called a "sea butterfly") found in Arctic waters is especially vulnerable to the acidification process. Whales, salmon, herring, and various seabirds dine on this little shellfish. Its disappearance would therefore have a major impact on the entire ocean food chain.

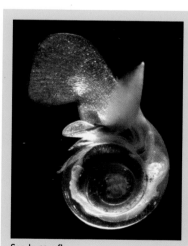

Sea butterfly.
Photo credit: NOAA

The cold-water coral species *Lophelia pertusa* is also extremely vulnerable to rising acidity. Reefs in the northern oceans are made up of only one or two kinds of coral, unlike tropical reefs, which are made up of many different kinds. The loss of *Lophelia pertusa* would therefore devastate coral reefs off the coasts of Norway and Scotland, damaging the habitats of dozens of fish species and other sea creatures.

# The Carbon Conundrum:
## Part #2—Climate Change

Like acidification, climate change is caused, in part, by humans pumping tons of carbon gas into the atmosphere. When CO2 and other greenhouse gases—nitrous oxide, methane, and ozone—are released into the air in large quantities, they create a barrier (like a blanket) around our planet that traps solar radiation and shoots it back to the earth. This causes the earth to slowly heat up, which messes with all kinds of things . . . including the ocean.

## The Global Conveyor Belt

When the ocean heats up during global warming, this affects how its currents flow. Currents operate according to a process called **thermohaline circulation**—or what is commonly known as the "global conveyor belt."

Here is what the ocean's conveyor belt looks like:

> **Thermohaline circulation** is the rising and sinking of ocean water driven by contrasts in water density, which is due in turn to differences in temperature and salinity.

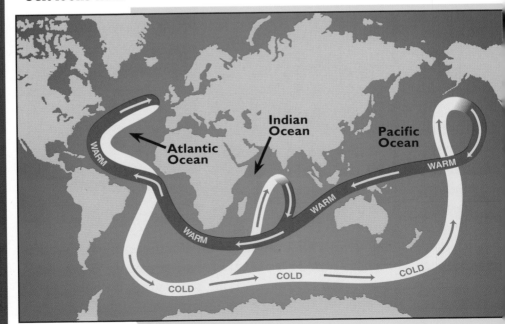

On the relatively warm surface of the ocean, wind moves the currents along. But currents flow at all depths of the ocean. The force that drives the current in deeper, colder water is water density, and the density is controlled by the water's temperature (thermo) and saltiness, or salinity (haline). Combine them and you have thermohaline circulation.

Here is how the ocean's conveyor belt operates:

1. Ice forms in the Polar Regions—forming "sea ice."

2. This ice forms using freshwater, leaving the salt behind and making the surrounding ocean water saltier.

3. The density, or weight, of the water gets heavier because of the salt and the water starts to sink.

4. The warmer water on ocean's surface has to replace the sinking water, and soon this water gets cold and salty and it, too, begins to sink.

5. This is the start of the deep-ocean currents driving the conveyor belt.

The global thermohaline circulation moves all over the ocean, from Antarctica to the equator to Africa, South America, North America, the Indian Ocean, and Pacific Ocean. It acts as a giant heating and air-conditioning system, providing warmth and cooling for our planet. For example, the sinking cold, salty, dense water in the North Atlantic Ocean helps draw warm surface waters northward. Heat from the ocean rises into the atmosphere above the North Atlantic Ocean, and winds carry the heat east making Europe warmer. In addition to our weather, this process also impacts our food sources. Cool, nutrient-rich waters support the growth of algae and seaweed, which is a key ingredient in the food chain we depend upon.

# time for
# REFLECTION

What have you already learned about oceans that you did not know before? What do you most want to remember? Who do you want to talk with about what you're learning? Share the news—be a voice for change!

# "I'm Melting!"

As you've likely heard, global warming is also causing Earth's glaciers to melt faster than predicted. In fact, by some estimates, Glacier National Park in Montana could be without glaciers by the year 2030, and the entire Arctic Ocean could be ice-free by 2040. What will all of this melting ice do to our rivers and lakes, oceans and shores? To our plants and animals? To our climate? To us?

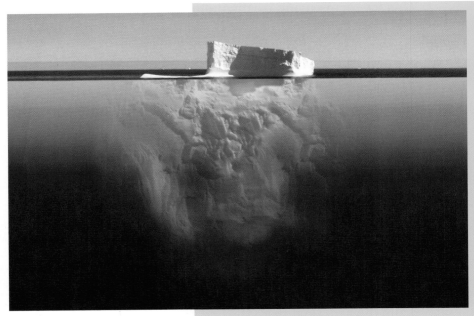

An iceberg visible above and below the water's surface.

Our Polar Regions are particularly susceptible to global warming. Arctic temperatures have been rising twice as fast as elsewhere in the world. On the Antarctic Peninsula, temperatures have increased five times faster. These regions are particularly sensitive to warming, in part, because of two persistent cycles:

Cycle #1: Ice and snow reflect the majority of the solar energy reaching the earth's surface, while ice-free surfaces absorb this energy. Snow and ice cover therefore have a cooling effect on the earth, but as they melt, more solar energy is absorbed, raising temperatures and melting even *more* ice.

Cycle #2: As ice melts in these regions, the permafrost (permanently frozen ground) thaws. Permafrost contains carbon that has been trapped in the soil since the last ice age, over a million years ago. As the permafrost melts, large quantities of carbon are released in the form of methane, a powerful greenhouse gas that increases global warming.

All this melting ice releases freshwater into the salty oceans, which can disrupt the thermohaline circulation, a.k.a. the global conveyor belt. Salty ocean water at high latitudes is becoming fresher as polar ice melts, and this lighter freshwater is not sinking and circulating through the deep ocean as it should. Given the current rate of change, scientists estimate that the global ocean conveyor belt may slow or stop altogether within the next few decades. This would have serious implications for countries in the northern hemisphere, as the warm surface waters in the Atlantic cease to be moved northward, and could eventually send Western Europe and North America into a deep freeze.

# The Power of Water

Pour water into your hands and it seems oh so gentle. Dive into a pool—how refreshing! Stand in the way of a typhoon, however, and you will experience the real power of water. How does ocean warming lead to these types of dangerous weather conditions? An increase in ocean temperatures, as we've seen, can disrupt the global thermohaline circulation, which in turn can affect the oceans' tides and storm systems. If humans continue down this destructive path, the hurricanes, typhoons, and other tropical storms will continue to increase in number, frequency, and intensity.

## time for
## REFLECTION

What natural disasters have been in the news lately? How might they confirm that our climate conditions are changing? Take the information from these pages and relate it to what's happening today in the world around you. Stay connected!

# Environmental Refugees

Populations migrate for various reasons: to find new jobs, to be closer to family, to escape war, to pursue an education, among many others. But did you ever think people would move because of climate change? A new term is being used for this phenomenon: *environmental refugees*. These are people forced to leave their homes due to the impact of global warming. Already about 2,400 of the 12,000 residents of Tuvalu, a tiny island nation in the South Pacific, have migrated primarily to New Zealand because of rising seas, more frequent dangerous storms, and the destruction of coral reefs that are the backbone of the islands. Other regions are being studied by scientists concerned with vulnerable populations, such as the deltas of Vietnam, the coast of Bangladesh, and the Sahel in Africa; these areas are faced with flooding, rising sea levels, or water shortages.

"It is interesting how often the impact of climate change is illustrated by talking about the problems the polar bears will face, rather than the much greater number of poor people who will die unless significant investments are made to help them."

—Bill Gates, founder of Microsoft, philanthropist

**YOUR TURN**

### Adopt a Threatened Area

Select a place in the world at risk of losing its very existence, like Tuvalu. Or choose a place that might succumb to drought, such as the African Sahel, or be destroyed by flooding, like the deltas in Vietnam. Learn all you can about the issue. Make a commitment to follow this area's progress over time. Discover different viewpoints and courses of action proposed by governments, local and outside communities, and area businesses. See how the media covers the story. Become an expert, and then share your knowledge with others.

# Plastics, Pollution, & Trash

Okay, so carbon pollution = ocean acidification + global warming = a huge problem. But carbon is certainly not the only thing we're dumping into our environment. A full 80 percent of pollution in the marine environment comes from land-based sources, such as chemical fertilizers, waste products, and litter.

Remember that granola bar wrapper you accidentally dropped on the ground over lunch? It might arrive at the beach before you do. Litter can travel to the ocean from many miles inland, blown by the wind or carried along by rivers and streams. We are all responsible for food wrappers, bottles, and bags in our waters. Overflowing sewage systems and storm drains add to the burden by ferrying trash from roads and streets to the sea. Marine debris these days includes mainly synthetic materials, such as plastics, where it once contained mostly organic materials. Items like packing straps, tarps, nets, and containers last for years and often travel thousands of miles on ocean currents.

Trash and plastic swirl through the world's oceans, leaving a trail of destruction. Plastic contains toxic chemicals, and as animals mistake the plastic for food, they are exposed to these toxins and many of them suffocate. Others starve to death from a

This sea lion became entangled in a gill net and was cut free. However, the monofilament lines around its head and neck were not removed. As the animal grew, the line cut a deep gash into its skin. Hundreds of thousands of sea lions and other wildlife become entangled in discarded fishing gear each year.

Photo credit: Marine Photobank from © 1990 Bob Talbot, LegaSea Project lack of nutrition. Even uneaten trash, like nets and plastic soda can rings, ensnares and kills thousands of creatures. Curious seals poke their noses into plastic containers and get stuck, preventing them from eating or even breathing. Playful dolphins swirl around discarded fishing rope, becoming entangled. When animals get caught in abandoned fishing nets, lines, and ropes in a phenomenon known as "ghost fishing," they may drown immediately or drag the debris around until they weaken and die. Nets drifting underwater can also snag on corals, sea fans, or sponges, damaging or destroying them.

Whenever possible, avoid buying six-packs of cans and bottles in plastic holders. If you do come across these holders, be sure to cut the plastic rings apart and dispose of them properly, so they don't end up ensnaring an animal by accident.

EARTH**ECHO**
INTERNATIONAL

# TEENS IN ACTION

## Worldwide
### Coastal Cleanup Day

During the 2008 Ocean Conservancy Coastal Cleanup Day, volunteers from 100 countries and 42 U.S. states picked up an astounding 6.8 million pounds of trash along an estimated 17,000 miles of coastline. Of the 43 specific items tallied, from light bulbs to fishing line, the top three items recorded were cigarette butts (3.2 million), plastic bags (1.4 million), and food wrappers/containers (943,000). In all, 11.4 million items were collected. All these things can be easily contained if people dispose of them carefully. Here are surprising statistics from the project:

- The total weight of garbage collected matched the weight of 18 blue whales.

- Volunteers rounded up 26,585 tires—enough for 6,646 cars, and one spare!

- Volunteers found 509,593 drinking straws and stirrers, which stacked end-to-end would be nearly 12 times the height of Mt. Everest.

- Every year, thousands of marine mammals, sea turtles, seabirds, and fishes are injured or killed because of encounters with common items that we carelessly throw away.

# The Great Pacific Garbage Patch

Yuck! The Great Pacific Garbage Patch, Trash Island, Plastic Soup—whatever you call it, there's one heck of a garbage dump floating out in our ocean. Located between Hawai'i and California, it's twice the size of Texas. The mass has been growing since the 1950s, and unless people intervene, this hunk of junk will continue to collect more and more waste—including discarded electronics, children's toys, and most of all, tons of nonbiodegradable plastic.

Map showing how trash enters the ocean along the Pacific coast. The trash swirls in two main vortices: the western Pacific Garbage Patch (on left) and the eastern Pacific Garbage Patch (on right).

Of this giant heap, 40 percent is plastic—evidence that humans are doing a lousy job of properly disposing of the 260 million tons of plastic we create every year. We only recycle 5 percent of that amount. With the garbage patch sprawling in international waters, no country is willing to take responsibility for the massive cleanup necessary. This leaves independent researchers to imagine solutions. One organization, Project Kaisei, suggests harnessing the energy stored in the plastic to create fuel. In

**Does Plastic Biodegrade?**
The vast majority of plastic does not biodegrade, or break down into natural elements, like organic materials do. At least not for 1,000 years or more. Rather than biodegrade, plastic *photodegrades*—it breaks into tiny toxic bits. These fragmented particles called "nurdles" cause further problems by being ingested as food by jellyfish and other marine life and thus moving up the food chain.

the meantime, other researchers are tracking the movement of debris making its way into this trash island.

Environmental stewards remind consumers that one long-term solution is to change the way our plastics are made. Look for the BPI (Biodegradable Products Institute) logo when deciding what to buy—these products are *compostable* (able to be composted and broken down into natural elements).

One thing is for certain: If left alone to circulate in our oceans, this garbage will continue to permanently harm the natural environment and contaminate our food supply with the toxins of our own waste.

An estimated 2.4 million pounds of plastic pollution enter the world's oceans *every hour.* How much trash do you make as one person? Could you make less? Here are some quick ideas to start with:

- Buy products contained in less packaging
- Buy compostable products whenever possible, and follow your city's recycling guidelines
- Use a reusable cloth bag when shopping

**YOUR TURN**

**Want to know more about the Great Pacific Garbage Patch? Visit these sites:**

**Sea Lab:** www.algalita.org/sea_lab. The Algalita Marine Research Foundation in Southern California operates a Sea Lab to process the samplings of trash picked up on their ocean excursions. Sea Lab also has an Environmental Charter High School program where students research beach sand to determine the amount of plastic particles in it, called the "plastic load."

**NOAA's Marine Debris Program:** marinedebris.noaa.gov. The Marine Debris Program is part of the National Oceanic and Atmospheric Administration (NOAA), a division of the U.S. government. The program has funded and helped support over 140 projects working with partners and addressing marine debris across the nation.

---

"There are no boundaries on the real Planet Earth. No United States, no Soviet Union*, no China, no Taiwan . . . Rivers flow unimpeded across the swaths of continents. The persistent tides—the pulse of the sea—do not discriminate; they push against all the varied shores on Earth."—*Jacques Cousteau, explorer*

---

*The Soviet Union ceased to exist in 1991 and the area now includes Russia and several other Eurasian countries.

# time for
# REFLECTION

Who's in charge here? Since all the world's waterways are interconnected, can any nation's government look at the Great Pacific Garbage Patch and say, "That's not our problem"? How should we think about national boundaries when it comes to water?

# Runoff Pollution

Runoff pollution is toxic liquid flowing from the land into waterways from septic tanks, cars, trucks and boats, farms, ranches, and freshwater areas. This waste often makes river, lake, and ocean water unsafe for humans and wildlife.

In the United States, more than one-third of the waters are adversely affected by coastal pollution. In some areas, runoff pollution is so bad that beaches need to be closed following rainstorms. Drinking water supplies can be contaminated by polluted runoff liquid, as can coastal waters containing valuable fish populations. Experts think there is a link between agricultural runoff and water-borne organisms that cause lesions and death in fish. Humans who come in contact with these polluted waters and infected fish can also experience harmful symptoms, such as intestinal illnesses and lead poisoning.

Millions of car and truck engines make miniature "oil spills" every day onto roads and parking lots, which add significantly to runoff pollution. Some water pollution actually starts as air pollution, which settles into waterways and oceans. In addition, top soil or silt from fields or construction sites can trickle into waterways, harming fish and wildlife habitats.

Correcting the harmful effects of runoff pollution is costly. Each year millions of dollars are spent to restore and protect areas damaged or endangered by these pollutants.

- Well-fertilized lawns may be contributing to fertilizer runoff pollution in your area. When you mow your own or your neighbors' lawns, let the lawn fertilize itself (or "self-mulch") by leaving grass clippings on the ground instead of raking them off.
- A lot of agricultural runoff pollution comes from farms growing grain crops to feed the livestock that provides your hamburger or steak dinner. Could you give up one meat dinner a week? It would help cut down on the need for these grain crops . . . and it's good for you!
- The EPA estimates that "every three weeks, more oil is deposited on driveways and streets in the United States than the Exxon Valdez Oil spill in Alaska." Advise your family to keep cars in good running order—even small oil leaks should be fixed quickly.

EARTH**ECHO**
INTERNATIONAL

# TEENS IN ACTION

## Gishwati, Rwanda
*Bamboo Buffers*

Students in Rwanda also addressed runoff pollution. The Rwanda University Club for Conservation of Biodiversity created a buffer zone in the Gishwati Forest Reserve in the Western province of Rwanda, in connection with the Gishwati Area Conservation Program. They planted bamboo trees in the buffer zone to separate human activities such as agriculture and farming from the Gishwati Forest Reserve and prevent runoff pollution. During this experience, students learned about the importance of reversing environmental damage by planting vegetation to counterbalance the negative effects of human activity.

## West Branch, Iowa, United States
*Team Deadweight*

By joining the Siemens We Can Change the World Challenge (www.wecanchange.com), Team Deadweight from West Branch Middle School identified and responded to a community environmental need. What need did they discover? Lead weight wheels—the weights attached to tires for stabilization. These weights frequently fall off cars, making them one of the biggest sources of poisonous lead released into our land and water. When a student observed his father, an auto mechanic, throwing away these lead weights, his team found their issue: "Is lead weight disposal regulated? If not, what's the environmental risk and what can be done?" With the help of their science teacher, students discovered that lead weights are not regulated and began gathering data about how much lead is deposited into the environment. They then created a campaign to replace the lead weights with steel ones.

Can kids living in "land-locked" areas such as the Midwestern United States help save the oceans? You bet they can. Just ask the students of Team Deadweight! By helping to eliminate a significant source of lead pollution in the environment, these students have taken a huge step toward cleaner lakes, rivers, and oceans.

Team Deadweight presented to their City Council, Community School District, and other local civic organizations. The city and school districts were convinced and agreed to phase out lead wheel weights in vehicles owned by the city and school districts. In addition, the students teamed with several legislators to develop three bills proposing to phase out the harmful metal citywide, and even presented to the Environmental Protection Agency (EPA), which is now considering a similar ban of lead wheel weights nationwide.

**"We all live upstream from one another. No matter where you live, your actions affect our world's oceans and waterways."**
—Philippe Cousteau

# Coral Reefs in Crisis

One of the most visible and troubling effects of human treatment of the oceans can be seen in coral reefs, one of the ocean's most prized inhabitants. The amazing hues, intricate shapes, and thousands of fish make healthy coral reefs spectacular underwater places to visit. They are the most biologically diverse areas in the world, more diverse even than rainforests. And each reef is completely unique in its form and the kinds of animals it hosts. A large number of plants and animals that live in coral reefs have not even been studied or named yet. Some of the ones we are studying now—and have yet to study—may give us new medicines to treat cancer, antibiotics to fight infections, and protection from harmful solar rays.

Coral reefs may resemble a sort of plant life, but they are actually formed by coral polyps, which are tiny animals that live in colonies. Each coral polyp builds a little shell, or apartment, for itself out of limestone. Together, the coral polyp colony builds an entire neighborhood of stony apartments stacked on top of one another. Every generation of coral polyp builds a new layer of limestone on top of the last. The nooks and crannies in this intricate neighborhood provide places for other animals such as all types of fish, sponges, sea stars, anemones, turtles, mollusks, crustaceans, snails, sea snakes, and plants to live and visit.

Six major physical factors affect coral reef development:

1. Water temperature

2. Water depth

3. Amount of sunlight penetrating the water

4. Water salinity (saltiness)

5. Amount of sediment in the water

6. Emergence into air (reefs do not like to be exposed to air)

As our ocean water changes, these factors change, causing coral reefs to suffer and sometimes disappear altogether. The main culprits threatening coral reefs are global warming, ocean acidification, erosion, pollution, fishing, and tourism.

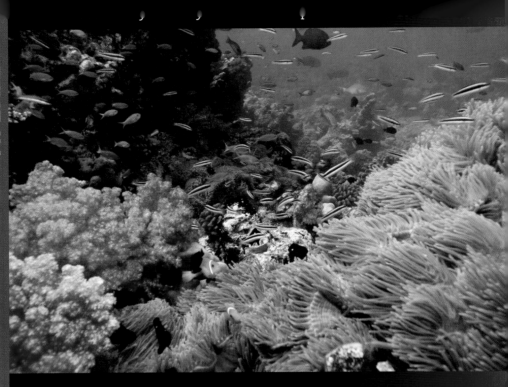

Now, imagine this reef just all white. Colorless.

"One way to open your eyes is to ask yourself, 'What if I had never seen this before? What if I knew I would never see it again?'"—Rachel Carson, environmentalist and author of *Silent Spring*

# Global Warming

As carbon pollution and global warming causes the ocean water to heat up to higher than normal temperatures, the coral reefs are becoming bleached. All the beautiful colors? Gone. The algae that live inside the coral polyps in a reef are what give coral reefs their brilliant colors. As the water warms, this algae can die off, causing an entire reef to turn white, or "bleach." A few days after bleaching, the coral reef will darken and die.

# Ocean Acidification

A more acidic ocean affects the mineral called carbonate that the shellfish and corals use to create their shells. Increasing acidification slows the growth of the carbonate and weakens the corals' shells. If pH levels drop enough, the shells will literally dissolve, leaving behind no skeletons, which means no reef.

# Erosion and Pollution

During the erosion process, silt, mud, fertilizers, and herbicides that wash off the surrounding land into the sea damage delicate coral reefs. The silt and mud cover the corals in a haze. Fertilizers and untreated sewage release an excess of nutrients into the water, causing certain types of algae to explode in growth, choking the reefs. In addition, oil spills in the ocean suffocate living corals and poison the water around them. It can take many years for a reef community to recover from the damage of a single oil spill.

# Fishing and Tourism

Humans have done a great deal of damage to coral reefs around the world, particularly the fishing and tourism industries. Factory-fishing vessels that trawl the seafloor often bulldoze right over reefs, destroying an entire underwater neighborhood in a single blow. To attract cruise ships, some coastal communities have literally blasted through the reefs to create boat channels. Divers and snorkelers damage or break fragile coral branches by simply touching them or grazing them with a careless hand or flipper. Dive boat operators and fishers destroy reefs with anchors and propeller blades. Souvenir-seeking tourists snag pieces of coral, which took the reef years to build and may disrupt the delicate reef ecosystem.

**YOUR TURN**

**A Slogan for the Waters**
Many parts of the world depend on tourism for local livelihood. Yet tourists can sometimes be careless and are often oblivious contributors to water-related problems. What risks or threats does tourism present in your community? Start a campaign to raise awareness of the need to respect our waters and shorelines. Many national parks and forests have slogans like "Leave No Trace" and "Take Only Pictures, Leave Only Footprints" to remind visitors of the care needed to preserve natural areas. What's your slogan to protect a waterway that matters to you? Be creative. Get the word out—use your voice!

Is your family planning a vacation? Talk to your parents about choosing eco-friendly lodging and tour operators. Visit www .friendsofworldheritage.org or www.ecotourism.org for more information.

EARTH**ECHO**
INTERNATIONAL

## What Can Be Done to Save Our Reefs?

Here are three primary ways people can help:

- Help stop climate change and OA by reducing our $CO_2$ emissions. This means using more efficient cars such as hybrids, and using responsible wind, solar, and hydro (water) energy wherever possible.

- Lobby to create protected areas in the ocean known as marine sanctuaries. Examples of marine sanctuaries include the Monterey Bay National Marine Sanctuary in the United States and the Saguenay–St. Lawrence Marine Park in Canada.

- Campaign to improve fishing practices so that nets do not drag along the bottom of the ocean and destroy the fragile coral reefs.

Mural on a building in St. Thomas, U.S. Virgin Islands.

# TEENS IN ACTION

## Tavernier, Florida, United States
### Operation Coral Restoration

Coral Shores High School marine science teacher David Makepeace beams as his students explain their coral restoration service learning efforts. "If we don't help the coral out now, they could be gone in our lifetime," says Zach Pardo, a senior who plans to study marine biology. "Do you know there are more than 3,500 corals in the nursery now, and we helped with most of them?" asks senior Jenna Regelmann.

The coral restoration nursery, set up and managed by Coral Restoration Foundation (CRF), is in 30 feet of water more than three miles offshore in the Florida Keys. Since 2003, more than 160 Coral Shores students have assisted at CRF's coral nursery and various restoration sites around the Upper Keys. Some students lead student and adult volunteer groups and make presentations for conferences and civic organizations. Despite the time commitment and physical demand, they can't seem to get enough of the coral restoration work. "Field science, especially underwater, is a lot more glamorous on TV than in real life," observes Makepeace. "The work can be exhausting but the lure of this good work usually results in more kids signing up than the twelve passenger boat will carry. I'll admit the idea of SCUBA diving during school time is enticing as well."

Coral Shores High School students measuring new coral growth. Photo credit: David Makepeace

Senior Dannon Magrane explains: "Our marine studies class has our own coral transplanting site. We mount, clean, and transplant the corals. Transplanting corals means removing corals from propagation modules and relocating them to a coral reef where they can grow. We dive into the water and meet with our groups down on the nursery site. Each group has a propagation module and transplanting discs. We affix the discs onto the module while we wait for our coral cuttings. Then we affix the corals to the disc on a smooth point on the reef. We keep records of every transplanted coral. Then, we grab our cleaning tools and clean older corals by scraping algae off the discs. Certain types of algae prevent the coral from growing and that is why cleaning the coral is so important. Everything we do is to save the coral. I can come back in years to come and see how they have grown."

" For as long as I can remember, my father has been telling me what a beautiful place the Keys was when he was a kid and how it has changed. In my 18 years, I have seen a decline. I want to try to preserve as much as possible of what is left. "
—*Malley Burmaster, age 18*

The students also restore seagrass, monitor reef growth, and conduct fish counts. They even venture into advocacy. They have addressed state officials about the importance of maintaining the

## Sensitive Seagrass

Photo credit: NOAA

Seagrass is a shallow saltwater plant. It's similar to coral reefs because it, too, provides shelter, food, and water purification. Young fish, turtles, anemones, and other ocean animals use seagrass beds as places to live, eat, and hide from predators. Seagrass is very susceptible to the changes in its environment because it needs light more than any other plant in the world. Seagrass sensitivity and reactions inform scientists of ocean changes and may help them predict future ocean trends.

Florida Keys National Marine Sanctuary. And when they grew troubled by widespread algae blooms in Florida Bay, they spoke to the South Florida Water Management District Governing Board about the need for continued restoration in the Everglades, which affect the algae blooms.

A student gathering data.
Photo credit: David Makepeace

Students in the Coral Shores Marine Studies Program receive a high school science credit through a combination of assessments including reflections, PowerPoint portfolios, video products, written reports, and presentations. Their partner organizations include the Coral Restoration Foundation, Florida Fish and Wildlife Conservation Commission Research Institute, Reef Environmental Education Foundation, and the Monofilament and Recovery and Recycling Program. New service efforts are planned when students identify a need or community members contact them.

Originally, the class began when students in a service club and their teacher, Mr. Makepeace, became concerned about nearby water quality issues. He explains, "Soon students were doing water testing and the curricular links became obvious." The following year the Marine Studies Program was part of the curriculum. Projects have come and gone as needs and interests changed. "What remains consistent," says Makepeace, "is that this is about the kids and the ocean."

## Be a Change Agent

**YOUR TURN**

This book is all about change—how the planet is changing due to global warming and ocean acidification, how weather patterns and food chains change, and most importantly, how students become agents of *good* change. Find a story of someone who already has taken action in your community to improve the environment. What was the motivation? How did the community respond? What lessons were learned? Knowing the history of change in your community can be helpful in developing your own action plans. History *matters*—as you will see in the next section.

# Looking Back: Historical Moments & Actions

What can history tell us about our oceans? How have humans helped and harmed our waterways in the past? Read about some of the champions and significant events that have shaped our water world today.

## A Brief History of Ocean Exploration

### Early Explorers

The earliest sea explorers rarely ventured out of sight of land. The Polynesians and Phoenicians were first to develop open sea routes. The Polynesians used sophisticated celestial observation to travel among the islands of the South Pacific. Historians believe the Phoenicians sailed from the Mediterranean Sea to the shores of present-day England by 600 BC. As boats grew sturdier, seafarers ventured farther from home, creating maps that detailed water currents and physical land features.

### The Age of Exploration

Europe's Age of Exploration is often attributed to Prince Henry of Portugal, also known as Henry the Navigator. During the 1400s, his devotion to exploring led to mapping the coast of Western Africa, which resulted in valuable trade routes around the Cape of Good Hope and into the Indian Ocean. Then in 1492, an explorer named Christopher Columbus traveled west to the "New World," using the charts built by his predecessors. With accumulated data about coastal topography, winds, waves, and currents, Ferdinand Magellan sailed a full circle around Earth in 1520. Before and during these travels by Europeans, native peoples throughout the Americas and the Arctic ventured offshore as well, pioneering elaborate trade networks along the coastlines and making efficient use of abundant marine resources.

# LEGENDS OF THE SEA

Ancient Greek legends and myths acknowledge the bond between human fortune and the sea. In one famous story, Polykrates, a wealthy builder, casts his most precious object into the sea to avoid the wrath of the gods who might be jealous of his good fortune. But the ring he throws away returns to him in the belly of a fish! Folklore also reveals a deep bond between dolphins and people. Ancient Greeks believed that dolphins loved music and helped fishermen. There are countless tales of young boys being saved by dolphins. In one account, a dolphin carried a child to school every day. Soon after the child died and stopped coming back to the sea, the dolphin perished out of sorrow.

The sea was also feared, due to the frequency of shipwrecks. The sea's often overwhelming power was embodied by the wrathful "earth-shaker" Greek god Poseidon. Historical stories of traversing the sea, like that of Homer's *The Odyssey*, are filled with accounts of monsters, beasts, and fatal temptations. Even when the sea is considered a playground of fantastical and destructive forces, it proves a resource for the imagination.

## Into the Deep

In the mid 1500s, interest in what was below the waves swept through Europe. With crude helmets and diving bells (airtight chambers), early explorers could spend short periods of time underwater. These devices allowed humans to glimpse at plants and fish that were not visible from the surface. Scientists quickly realized that a lot more was going on down there than anybody knew. Continued advances were made with submersible boats able to delve 12 feet below sea level, assisted by air hoses attached to floats at the surface.

## Oceanography Comes of Age

During the 20th century, ship technology changed dramatically. Wartime antisubmarine systems spurred the development of sonar devices, which used underwater sound waves to detect enemy ships. These wartime systems were later refined to assist in the mapping of the deep ocean and the sea floor, and allowed scientists to research and photograph shipwrecks, such as the *Titanic*.

Today, remote-controlled robotic vehicles can go where humans cannot and collect data and samples in trenches that are miles beneath the ocean's surface.

The excitement of ocean exploration is ongoing, because there's so much left to discover!

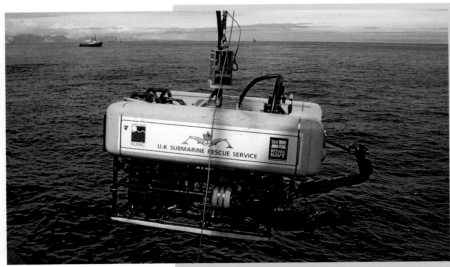

A British Scorpio underwater robot.
Photo credit: © Handout/British Ministry of Defence/Jonathan Holloway/Reuters/Corbis

# Captain Jacques Cousteau— Adventurer, Visionary, and Steward

Photo credit: © Bettmann/Corbis

> **"The best way to observe a fish is to become a fish."**—Jacques Cousteau

For millennia, explorers traveled the earth's oceans in search of new lands, unfamiliar cultures, and exotic forms of life. Jacques Cousteau, born in southwest France, spent his life traveling these same seas, not in search of the life on its surface, but to discover what lay beneath. His groundbreaking work taught the world that the oceans are vital to our existence, that "water and life are indissolubly bound." He revealed the mystery and majesty of these underwater worlds by building bridges to take us there. In 1943, Cousteau and the engineer Emile Gagnan invented the Aqualung, a wearable oxygen tank (later to become known as SCUBA gear), which allowed for easier and safer diving. He outfitted his boat, the *Calypso,* with his own innovative technologies like the diving saucer and underwater cameras.

With more than 16 books and films admired by the public and critics alike, Cousteau won three Academy Awards for the documentaries *The Silent World* (1957), *Le Poisson Rouge* (1959), and *World Without Sun* (1965). These films showed the world that rather than fearing the sea and its creatures, like sharks and whales, we must celebrate this thriving ecosystem. He was the first filmmaker to capture the exuberant experience of scuba diving.

Cousteau's visionary project opened up new worlds for countless future explorations, bringing underwater sights to us all. He hoped that understanding and valuing our intimate connection with the ocean would foster a more caring relationship and inspire innovation, such as harnessing the ocean's tides and temperatures to solve Earth's energy crisis. He imagined the day when humans would cultivate their food on the sea floor and was the first person to create an underwater human settlement.

Jacques Cousteau was one of the 20th century's greatest adventurers. He united his love of technology and exploration in revolutionary ways to teach people about their intimate connection to the bodies of water covering the earth's surface. His dream: that we will all continue to care for our oceans as the tremendous source of life that this Water Planet truly is.

Do you love the underwater world? Get closer to it by swimming with goggles and a snorkel. If you want to try diving, look for a SCUBA certification class near you. Often, you will first train in a swimming pool and then graduate to a lake or coastal area.

**SCUBA = S**elf **C**ontained **U**nderwater **B**reathing **A**pparatus

EARTH**ECHO**
I N T E R N A T I O N A L

Jacques Cousteau demonstrates his latest invention, the Aqualung. October 1950.

# Dr. Sylvia Earle: Legendary Oceanographer

> "Many of us ask what can I, as one person, do, but history shows us that everything good and bad starts because somebody does something or does not do something."—Sylvia Earle

Photo credit: © Macduff Everton/Corbis

Like Jacques Cousteau, ocean expert Sylvia Earle was not born along an ocean coast. Instead, she grew up on a New Jersey farm, and came to love nature, wilderness, and exploring. These interests combined to form her life's work: exploring and protecting "the blue heart of the planet"—our waters. The first in her family to go to college, Sylvia studied botany, which she believed was necessary to understanding ecosystems. After marrying and having children, she remained dedicated to understanding and exploring the oceans.

Learning to scuba dive was a critical step that led Sylvia to participate in numerous research projects all over the world. She led the first team of women *aquanauts* to live in an underwater research station off the coast of the Virgin Islands for two weeks. Dive after dive, Sylvia has provided research that has helped people understand the ocean floors, the impact of human conflicts and wars on oceans, and the need for marine animal protection. She has spent more than 7,000 hours conducting research underwater, and continues as an explorer today. Sylvia Earle transformed her childhood love of the outdoors originating on her family farm into a true spirit of discovery that benefits humans everywhere.

An *aquanaut* (similar to a "water astronaut") is a scuba diver who remains in an underwater habitat on the seafloor conducting research for an extended time period, usually 24 or more continuous hours.

# Animal Lifeguards:

## Eugenia Clark: The Shark Lady

Some children are content to observe fish in an aquarium. Eugenia Clark, however, visited a New York aquarium at age nine and grew up to actually *swim* with sharks. The shark fascinated her: "I was completely attached to it and I just thought, 'If only I could be in the water with a shark.'" Eugenia followed this passion to study fish, or ichthyology. Her specialty was the behavior, ecology, and taxonomy (classification) of fish, those fish we often consider the most dangerous and mysterious of marine creatures: sharks. As an ichthyologist and authority on sharks of all kinds—whale sharks, six-gill sharks, dusky sharks, thresher sharks, reef sharks, and others—Eugenia has spent more than 30 years diving with sharks to learn what attracts them, what repels them, and other behaviors. In fact, she has even hitched a ride on the back of a whale shark! After holding on for a while she finally let go, "But I was so sorry to let go of the most wonderful ride I've ever had in my life." She hopes others will join her in learning about these misunderstood animals and help save them from extinction.

## Archie Carr: The Turtle Guy

Archie Carr protected turtles. A zoologist, ecologist, and conservationist, his work extended to many animal species, yet his dedicated efforts to understand and document the lives of sea turtles charted new territory. Growing up in Savannah, Georgia, Archie had a backyard filled with cages of snakes, lizards, and turtles. Yet it was in the coastal areas of the Caribbean, the Americas, east Africa, and Australia that Archie tracked sea turtle migration and navigation. He took a firm stand against commercial sea turtle "ranching" and the removal of sea turtles from the endangered species list. He led Operation Green Turtle, which distributed turtle eggs and hatchlings to protected beaches, to save turtle populations from the brink of extinction. Archie made a tremendous influence through his studies, his activism, his teaching, and his tireless efforts to establish places where turtles still thrive today.

---

"For most of the wild things on Earth, the future must depend upon the conscience of mankind."—Archie Carr

# Making History Today: Movers & Shakers

We tend to think about history as only in the past, however, history is actually in the making at every moment. So who are today's history makers?

## Alexandra Cousteau: Emerging Explorer

Photo credit: BLUE LEGACY INTERNATIONAL

According to Philippe Cousteau's sister, Alexandra, she has "the coolest job description in the world: explorer." As the granddaughter of Jacques Cousteau and founder of Blue Legacy International and an "emerging explorer" for National Geographic, Alexandra joins others in redefining what exploration means in the 21st century. With most of our planet's land already observed, traversed, and inventoried, how can this term be defined for a new era and remain meaningful, new, and exciting? According to Alexandra, today an explorer might "explore an issue or see a place through new eyes. While there are not many places I can go for the first time, I can explore them through new ideas and parameters, and with new innovative tools."

The purpose of modern exploration has a new dimension—inspiring people to take care of the places we already know. For Alexandra, this involves viewing our environment through a specific lens: the water cycle. "From the top of Mount Everest to the deepest oceans and all the way around," she explains, "we live within a continuous flow of water. The water from the Ganges in India could rain over the plains of Kenya, end up in a cup of tea in the Queen's castle, or fill a swimming pool in a Dallas suburb. When we know this, we may behave differently and take action in our own lives."

What does a modern explorer's life entail? "Every day is different. Some days I curl up on my couch reading and doing research. I might be at an airport traveling to a speaking engagement. Sometimes I start early with my film crew on an expedition investigating human and natural elements of water. We work to tell the story of our water planet. We aim to shape society's dialogue to include water as one of the defining issues of our century by illustrating the interconnectedness of all water issues. We may have challenges and stress as well as moments of elation and triumph. But while not always easy, the work is always exciting. Our work is meant to add to our global conversation about important matters in a way that leads people toward action."

Explore with Alexandra two spectacular water systems:

## THE MANDATORY MEKONG

"In Cambodia we traveled the Mekong River to the Tonle Sap Lake, the largest lake in Southeast Asia. Every year in May, the river flow reverses because the Mekong cannot absorb all the water. Over three months, the lake floods and the entire area transforms. To adapt, people live in floating communities. There are entire villages with homes on platforms, and churches and fuel stations all on boats! People travel from place to place by boat. The surrounding forests flood to the treetops. The birds and cats and otters move to dry areas at the tops of trees. With the forest floods, the fish have lots of food from drowning insects.

All fish are spawning during this time, and the baby fish can hide in the branches of trees. When the dry season comes, the lake recedes and these now larger fish move down the Mekong—in a "direct delivery" food system to support people all along the river. As industry starts to build dams on the Mekong, one of the largest inland food ecosystems in the world will

A modern and an old house on the Mekong River near Battambang, Cambodia.

be disrupted. Along this river and lake, everyone depends on hundreds of fish species unique to Cambodia. These people function with and rely on nature."

## THE MIGHTY MISSISSIPPI

Back in the United States, the Mississippi River attracts Alexandra's explorer's eye, especially since this 2,340-mile river and its tributaries reach 31 states and two Canadian provinces. "The Mississippi, or Huck Finn's river, has importance historically, culturally, industrially, and agriculturally, and supports human, animal, and plant life as it flows to the Gulf of Mexico. And *all* is threatened. Pollution caused by farms—in Minnesota, Iowa, Tennessee, and Arkansas, to name a few—from over-fertilization and waste from other industries dumps excessive nutrients into the Mississippi. A quart of motor oil carelessly tossed down a drain in Montana, Pennsylvania, or Missouri joins with all the other garbage to create a dead zone in the Gulf of Mexico the size of New Jersey— about 7,000 square miles. Shrimp are jumping out of the water onto the beaches trying to breathe due to *eutrophication*. The fishermen who depend on the region can't make a living anymore. We have to reverse this through deliberate actions."

> *Eutrophication* is a concentration of chemicals that increases the growth of plankton and depletes the water of oxygen, which harms dependant life forms.

Alexandra observes, "In both of these locales, we depend on rivers and their tributaries for our health and well-being. Our actions can either make these resources scarce or incapable of supporting life, *or* they can reflect that our lives depend on water."

Visit Alexandra's website for more information: www.alexandracousteau.org.

"If there is magic on this planet, it is contained in water. It is life."
—Alexandra Cousteau, explorer

BLUE
LEGACY

**So You Want to Be an Explorer?**
Start by exploring your own watershed. Canoe around it. Hike around it. Explore with a camera, a journal, or a film or audio recorder. Make podcasts. Map your watershed, take photos, and post the images online. Talk about what you see and what changes you think need to be made. Bring what you see to the attention of your school, local officials, and community representatives. Use the information you discover to inspire other people to explore and take action. Become a leader and a role model for others.

## Alex Lin: Modern Innovator

"In fifth grade I was part of a school community problem-solving program, and we wanted to find an issue that mattered," said Alex Lin. "In 2004, I brought in a newspaper article about the e-waste (electronic waste) problem, which became larger than a one-year project. We chose this topic for the WIN Team— Westerly Innovations Network—formed by me and some of my friends."

Alex Lin is now a high school senior in Westerly, Rhode Island, and he explains in vivid detail the process his WIN Team followed:

"We read about the national e-waste issue and began conducting research to see the local need and what was already being done. We did surveys and interviews with local recycling companies; these came in handy when it came time to set up the recycling program. We approached the City Council and there was no method for recycling e-waste. Then a WIN Team member's neighbor was going to dump about 50 computers in the trash. This large-scale situation propelled us into action to make a sustainable plan. We sought to show our town a model system that could be replicated in other areas."

The WIN Team established three priorities: **Recycle, Refurbish,** and **Legislate**.

## RECYCLE

"We realized we needed sustainability that would come from a recycling receptacle in the town—a permanent transfer station that reliably disposes of electronics," said Lin. "When someone gets a new computer, usually they throw the old one away. When computers are discarded in landfills, the lead, cadmium, and other heavy minerals soak into the groundwater. We installed a receptacle at the transfer station that was provided by a local company that recycles electronics. This is an example of how partnerships are key to creating sustainable systems.

"Education is crucial. Many people don't know about the e-waste problem. At the beginning, based on our surveys, only about 13 percent of the local populace knew about proper disposal. Now it's about 100 percent. We presented to all the local elementary schools and gave them flyers and surveys to get back to us. We even had a lottery for returned surveys—the winner received a refurbished computer! We spoke to high schools and community groups, and wrote articles for newspapers about how people can get involved.

"We have now recycled over 300,000 pounds of electronic waste—an average of between 2,000–5,000 pounds a month."

## REFURBISH

"Refurbishing (repairing and reusing) electronics is about seven times more efficient than recycling because of the energy and resource consumption associated with recycling. Our efforts resulted in the refurbishing of over 300 computers to give to students. Who helped? Other students! We worked with our school's computer repair class and integrated computer refurbishing into their curriculum. The donated computers came from companies, banks, and individuals and went to local residents. Then we set our sights on distant places where young people lack electronic technology. We have WIN Children's Centers with computers in Sri Lanka, Mexico, Cameroon, and the Philippines—in places that need electronic technology."

## LEGISLATE

"How did we legislate? At first we did more research to know our materials inside and out, and also to learn about various electronic bills already created in other states. We met with local legislators because there was one such bill proposed in Rhode Island. We asked a lot of questions. We pushed for the bill, even testified. But the result was it did not pass.

"We regrouped and considered: Why didn't it pass? The language was too complicated. So I took the bill, simplified the wording into a resolution that we would propose to our town, get it passed there, and then expand it to the state level. The resolution was simple: Ban the dumping of electronic waste. Clear and concise. The town council of 2005 unanimously passed our proposal! No one in Westerly could dump their electronics. Then our Representative Peter Lewis took it to the state. We collected signatures for petitions to influence politicians. We testified before the environment committee. We gave a detailed presentation that was well received. We showed what 12- and 13-year-old kids can do!"

In 2006, the State of Rhode Island passed a bill that banned the improper disposal of e-waste. The WIN Team was instrumental in helping pass the bill. The law went into place in July 2007.

"We were determined. We would have testified again and again. In a certain way, kids have an almost louder voice than adults. When you find a topic you care about, do the hard work,

### Advice from Alex and the WIN Team

1. Make your plans and system sustainable.
2. Define the need.
3. Research and find partners.
4. Target your actions to where they are most useful.
5. Find the best solution with the greatest impact.

**Remember:** Being a young person usually works in your favor!

Read more about Alex and others like him in *Heroes of the Environment: True Stories of People Who Are Helping to Protect Our Planet* by Harriet Rohmer (Chronicle Books, 2009).

and find your voice, people will listen. Our voices are powerful."

Is Alex's work done now? Not a chance. WIN may soon become the World Innovations Network. Lin wants to influence a new generation. "We started in fifth grade, so now we are mentoring other fifth graders to get them started."

Do you know a young person like Alex who is making a difference in the world? Nominate her or him for a Brower Youth Award at www.broweryouthawards.org.

EARTH**ECHO**
INTERNATIONAL

## time for
# REFLECTION

Read this section again and think about how many careers are mentioned—from ocean explorer to politician to news reporter. Any career can have a connection to saving our oceans and waterways. What career do you have in mind? In what ways could you help our planet while in this profession?

## Summary

**P**reparation. In arming yourself with knowledge of the planet's interconnected water systems, you have prepared for action. You have chosen the need you want to address and learned as much background information as you could about it—including possible causes and solutions, what's been done in the past to meet this need, and what is being done today. Preparation extends beyond investigation by giving you the "big picture" of how every water issue you address affects every other, and the larger history and facts surrounding all of these issues.

# STAGE 3
## GET GOING→ACT

Knowledge prepares us and begins to generate ideas. Examples of what other young people have done help us start considering the planning process. All of this comes together as we move into the third stage of service learning and take *action to save our waters!*

# The Story of Tar Creek: Part #3
## Miami, Oklahoma, United States
(continued from page 60)

## How Did They Act?

The students published their research papers, poetry, and personal essays in two anthologies that tell their story, and they've given "toxic tours" to hundreds of other students and adults from the region to educate them about the Tar Creek Superfund site. They put up signs to keep kids out of the water and off the mounds of toxic dirt where they used to ride bikes. The students also hosted an annual conference that brought together state and national government officials, leaders of Native American groups, and members of the surrounding community to wrestle with the environmental and personal issues that resulted from the pollution.

The Story of Tar Creek continues on page 126.

# Your Little Choices Make a Big Splash

It's true: your daily choices and actions make all the difference to our planet's water system, whether or not you intend them to. Even your choices about things that may seem—on the surface—unrelated to water.

Our lifestyles include cars, fast food, disposable items (including paper plates and plastic sandwich bags), newspapers, air conditioning, cell phones, household appliances (such as microwaves and hairdryers), and many other items that make our lives safer, easier, and more comfortable. Unfortunately, pollution is often a consequence of producing, using, and disposing of these items. Waste is unwanted or discarded material. When waste is not contained, it is released into the environment and becomes pollution. Pollution generated by industries, agriculture, businesses, schools, vehicles, and even our homes if not properly handled, can contaminate our soil, water, and air. Once pollution is generated, it is pretty much here to stay. Even if it is eventually contained, pollution can meanwhile seep permanently into the earth's landscape, including our oceans and waterways.

When you plan your course of action, consider the following topics and the inspiring ways kids around the world are tackling them.

> **❝Everything you do makes a difference.❞**
> —Philippe Cousteau

## Electronics Recycling

Electronics are an integral part of our daily lives. Even in remote African villages people stay connected via cell phones, using solar chargers to reenergize batteries where there is no electricity. Electronic waste, or e-waste, accounts for *70 percent* of the toxic waste currently found in landfills. In addition to valuable metals like aluminum, electronics often contain hazardous materials like mercury, lead, or Freon. When placed in a landfill, even small doses of these materials can contaminate soil as well as drinking water. It is critical that these items—including cell phones, computers, televisions, air conditioners, microwaves, and others—be disposed of properly.

In the last section, you read about Alex Lin and his WIN Team's efforts to prevent e-waste, by recycling or refurbishing old computers and making it illegal for people to improperly dispose of their electronics. However, it also matters which electronics we choose to buy in the first place. With pressure from consumer groups, some manufacturers are starting to offer products intentionally designed to be easily disassembled so they can be easily refurbished and safely recycled.

Need the scoop on what and how to recycle? Check out www.earth911.com for facts and resources. Or go straight to www.wireflytradeins.com to turn in your old cell phones, game counsels, and electronics for cash or donations to your favorite nonprofit organizations (including EarthEcho International!).

EARTH**ECHO**
INTERNATIONAL

# Teens in Action

Minneapolis, Minnesota, United States
*Hazardous Chemicals? Not in My Water!*

How can families and communities learn about how the products they purchase affect their health and environment? Students in grades 6–8 at the Blake School in Minneapolis decided to teach them. They made an inventory of products in their homes, researched how hazardous the products were depending on their chemical content and their environmental effects if disposed of improperly, and then learned proper disposal methods. Students labeled these products in their homes and presented their research to families and other students in the community. Parents expressed amazement to learn they were using potentially toxic chemicals in their household, even in common cleaning products, and what their effects are on humans and other organisms in the surrounding environment.

The results of the Blake students' efforts? A community of smarter shoppers who know how to make informed decisions when purchasing household items and also when disposing of them. In the long run, these actions will increase the health of local waterways and send a message to manufacturers that consumers want environmentally friendly products.

What do vinegar, baking soda, lavender, and lemon juice have in common? These and other natural ingredients are used to create household cleansers that are safe and toxin-free. Search the Internet for recipes to make your own cleaning products. Remember, what you use in the shower goes down the drain, too. Choose shampoo and bath products that are phosphate-free, have low water content, and include minimal or recycled packaging.

EARTH**ECHO**
INTERNATIONAL

### Indianapolis, Indiana, United States
#### Bracelets for a Cause

Celebrities often wear ribbons, pins, or bracelets to promote causes they care about. Do you want to promote e-waste prevention, coastal restoration, or another "blue" cause? Make your own ribbon, pin, or bracelet. That's what teens in the Kiwanis Builders Club at Francis W. Parker Montessori School decided to do. To promote environmental action, they created "Support the Cause" bracelets made from recycled products. They wanted to be sure what they made would be biodegradable and wouldn't deplete our natural resources or put more plastic or oil-based products in our landfills. The bracelets have as their primary ingredients cardboard paper towel or toilet paper tubes, collage and art materials, and a heaping spoonful of creativity.

Photo credit: Michael S. Brooks

> " I like teaching my students that we can recycle and reuse materials to create beautiful art. Part of being creative involves seeing things in a different way. Using lessons that require recycling challenges students to think and rethink concepts and also emphasizes the importance of preserving our environment. "

—*Yvonne Whittaker, art teacher*

> " By taking care of our water in Indiana, like being sure industries are not polluting into our rivers, not letting plastic bags get into the water, and keeping our air clean, we will help keep fish and marine life from becoming extinct. The sea animals are important to our ecosystem and sustaining our oceans. "

—*Katie, age 12*

# Farming & Food

You probably have figured out by now that all Earth's ecosystems are interrelated. A soda straw that accidentally slips out of a person's hand in Idaho can end up along the beach in Mexico. Melting glaciers in the Arctic Circle can influence the rainy season in Bangladesh. And what you choose to eat for breakfast, lunch, and dinner has an effect on what a person in Kenya eats for breakfast, lunch, and dinner . . . or rather, what they might not have to eat.

Growing food, whether to produce rice for people or feed for livestock, requires vast quantities of water. In the United States alone, agricultural needs are the largest use of fresh water in the world. Every day 145 billion gallons of water is used to irrigate 62 million acres of cropland. This is three times the amount of water used by U.S. citizens' personal needs. For example, it takes about 400 gallons of water to produce one pound of wheat using current flood irrigation methods. One pound of rice requires about 900 gallons of water. One gallon of ethanol fuel from corn takes about 1,000 gallons of water. And to grow enough cattle feed grain to produce just one pound of beef takes about 2,000 gallons of water.

Due to water runoff from agricultural land, our streams, rivers, lakes, and oceans become polluted. The most common farming practices create serious water pollution by using vast amounts of

synthetic nitrogen-based fertilizers. This has become a major source of nitrous oxide, a greenhouse gas pollutant. And cows—they make enormous quantities of the greenhouse gas methane from their flatulence (you can figure out what that is).

What can farmers do? They can use other methods of farming that prove safer for our environment and the food on our tables. Perennial crops, crop rotation, non-tilling, and manure-based fertilizers can all reduce the pollution and soil erosion caused by farming. And methods like organic agriculture and composting produce fewer byproducts that harm the environment.

**Composting** is the process of using organic waste products to fertilize soil for gardening. You can compost wherever you live, even in an urban setting. Learn the basics at www.howtocompost.org and start composting at school and at home.

EARTH**ECHO**
INTERNATIONAL

## Overfishing

Humans are depleting the oceans of fish. Entire species of fish are being targeted and destroyed, disrupting the food chain from top to bottom and extensively impacting our ocean's ecosystems. For example, after decades of overfishing, the bluefin tuna population in the north Atlantic has declined 97% in the past 40 years. This fish has come to symbolize the misfortune of many large fish that are hunted until their massive numbers become so diminished they become endangered.

Overfishing happens when the number of fish caught exceeds the number of fish needed to sustain fish populations in a given region. Fishers endanger one species and then turn to another more plentiful species, thus continuing the decline of food supplies in the ocean. When fishers or consumers desire a particular species of fish, like bluefin tuna, they treat it as if it were unlimited. However, all of our natural resources, including ocean fish such as the bluefin tuna, are limited. As human populations grow and their demand for fish grows, supply will simply not meet demand. Some scientists estimate the loss of all major fisheries within 40 years unless something changes.

Too many fishing boats are on the ocean—especially large-scale, industrial vessels such as factory trawlers—with too much capacity for devastating fish populations and seafloor habitats such as coral reefs and sponges. To picture how many fish one factory trawler can catch at one time, imagine a net as large as four football fields. The bottom trawler drags heavy gates and traps across the seafloor, destroying the underwater terrain (including coral reefs), killing marine life as the net gathers every creature in its path, and then discarding the unwanted sea life.

"Imagine using a bulldozer to catch songbirds for food—that's what [bottom trawling] is like. After a trawler has gone by, [the sea floor] looks like a superhighway, it's just flat. Nobody's home. A few fish may swim in and out but the residents are just smothered, they're crushed. It's like paving them over."

—Sylvia Earle, oceanographer

Factory trawlers fish for pollack in the Bering Sea, Alaska.
Photo credit: © Natalie Fobes/Science Faction/Corbis

In the long term, overfishing can result in loss of jobs, lost biological diversity, and ecosystem collapse. Sustainable use of our oceans is crucial to human survival. Aquaculture (marine agriculture) may provide an alternative to the depletion of fish in the ocean and might have ecological and economic benefits to fisheries. Most important is saving the supply of fish in the ocean.

Do you like eating fish? That's fine, but if you want to make sure that fish still exist 40 years from now, choose *sustainable seafood* in restaurants and at your grocery store. Visit Blue Ocean Institute at www .blueocean.org/seafood for a list of the best options.

EARTH**ECHO**
I N T E R N A T I O N A L

### Fish Food Facts

- The earliest use of the oceans by humans was probably for food.

- Inshore waters have more productivity than most open-ocean waters and support larger populations of fish.

- Inshore fish populations started to decline in Europe during the 1300s.

- More people + more fishing = the reduction of many ocean fish populations.

"Not enough sustainable seafood currently exists in the world to supply the current demand. Not only must we choose sustainable seafood, we must cut our consumption considerably and stop eating and wasting so much of this precious resource."
—Philippe Cousteau

## Eating Local

Think about what you had for lunch. Did it come with a suitcase and a bus ticket? Actually, it probably did—you just can't see it. In the United States, most food travels about 1,200 miles before it lands on your plate. Pineapples from Hawaii, oranges from Florida, rice from Texas, maple syrup from Vermont, salmon from Alaska, peppers from Mexico, blueberries from Canada, and broccoli from China. Today most people have no idea where the food on their plate originated, much less how it was grown, even if it's labeled "organic." If you really want to know your food, the best way is to try to eat locally grown

Talk with your family about shopping at local farmers' markets and buying organic to reduce the use of pesticides. Visit www.localharvest.org to find farms and farmers' markets near you. Also stop by www.foodnews.org to download *The Shopper's Guide to Pesticides*— including the top "Dirty Dozen" fruits and veggies that you should try to buy organic.

EARTH**ECHO**
INTERNATIONAL

products. Whether a product is certified organic or not, any farming that minimizes the use of chemical fertilizers and pesticides is better for us and for our oceans. Many smaller farms that are not certified organic still use organic methods. The best way to know how good a farm's practices are for the planet is to talk to the farmer. Shake the hand that feeds you. Search out a local market and buy from a local farmer as often as possible.

**YOUR TURN**

### Eat Your Local Fruits and Veggies!

Where, oh where, does your food come from? Find out. Check with the school cafeteria, local market, and your favorite local restaurants. Are large supermarkets that truck in food the only option for your groceries? Or is there a farmers' market or food co-op near you where produce has been picked at local farms within the past 24 hours? Maybe there's even a community or school vegetable garden? Think of ways you can move the source of what you eat closer to home.

# Take Action

How to save our waterways and oceans? Get active. Get involved. Get others to join you. And take action! You have the facts, you have heard the call, and you have plenty of examples to get you inspired. So what will you do? Select one of the following actions or combine several—and get out there.

## Choose Your Kind of Action

- **Do It Now!** Get directly involved in recycling, restoring, and protecting.

- **Be a Message Maker.** Is social networking your game? Or do you envision large signs in your neighborhood reminding people to recycle or reuse household items? Communicate! Find creative ways to get out your message using public service announcements, posters, pamphlets, blogs, videos, and that all important *elevator speech*.

### WHAT'S YOUR ELEVATOR SPEECH?

Imagine you step into an elevator and the president of your country is there and says, "What's on your mind?" At most, you have about 30 seconds and 130 words to tell him or her. That's your "elevator speech." Have one ready!

- Know your key points—what you care about, what needs to happen, what you will do, and what others can do.

- Use short sentences that convey vivid images.

- Make solid eye contact.

- Mean what you say and say what you mean.

- **Join with Established Groups.** Who in your community would be delighted to have energetic young people helping out, sharing ideas, and getting things accomplished? Work alongside other people who care about the environment and our waters.

- **Raise Funds.** Keep in mind that any way you raise dollars for a charitable pro-ocean cause needs to respect the earth and our environment—and teach others along the way.

- **Walk the Talk.** Be a role model for others by making choices that show you care about our Water Planet.

- **Start a Campaign.** Get out there and campaign for your cause. One example of a campaign is *The Big Turn Off–Turn On!* Recruit others to turn off electronics that aren't being used and turn them on to riding bikes, which is good for their health *and* good for the environment.

**Holding a Fundraiser?** Make sure the funds you raise for an organization will go toward the cause you seek to support. Read the organization's literature. Do research about how they spend their dollars. Ask what percentages of their funds go directly to the important work that needs to be accomplished.

**Philippe Cousteau's Elevator Speech**

**1st floor:** Did you know that water is the single most important substance on the planet?

**2nd floor:** Water connects every being to one another—from drinking to energy production.

**3rd floor:** Water is quickly becoming the cause of the greatest crises of our century.

**4th floor:** I run a nonprofit called EarthEcho International, and we just launched the Water Planet Challenge.

**5th floor:** This Challenge empowers teens to bring about global change in our oceans and waterways.

**6th floor:** With cutting-edge technology, we can reach more than 25 million teens and keep track of the collective impact of all of their environmental projects.

**7th floor:** Are you ready to help? Here's what you can do . . . (*Hint:* Always have an idea about how the person you're talking to can get involved.)

- **Be Political.** The key to creating sustainable change is to become advocates—especially when our waters and their inhabitants can't speak for themselves. How have other adults and kids made their voices heard? What can young people do locally, nationally, and internationally to instigate necessary change?

  - Find out what your politicians think about and care about, and who on their political staff is responsible for environmental issues and causes.

  - Write letters to public officials when policy is being developed or when a topic deserves their attention.

  - Let your public officials know what you are doing—as you get started, along the way, and as your activities culminate. Invite them to be part of your team.

Read up on the people in your government who care about the environment. In the United States, visit League of Conservation Voters (www.lcv.org), and in British Columbia, Canada, visit Conservation Voters of BC www .conservationvoters.ca.

EARTH**ECHO**
INTERNATIONAL

"We have a stewardship responsibility to maintain healthy, resilient, and sustainable oceans, coasts, and Great Lakes resources for the benefit of this and future generations."—U.S. President Barack Obama

**YOUR TURN** **Who Are Your Political Change Makers?**
Government by the people, for the people: people means *you*. Know your local, state, or provincial representatives. Attend events where you can meet them and hear them speak. Ask questions about their stances on environmental issues—local water issues in particular. Tell them what you and other kids are up to. Keep a log of who is on the "blue" team (pro-oceans and waterways), and remember: you will vote one day!

# TEENS IN ACTION

## Santa Fe, New Mexico, United States
*Fighting Phosphates*

Meet Sachiko Cooper DaSilva, a guitar-playing eighth grader who knits, skis, and knows her phosphates. At the Santa Fe Girls School in New Mexico, Sachi joins other seventh and eighth graders in studying local water issues. For over seven years, students have been spending time along the Santa Fe River below the waste-water treatment plant. On the nine-acre PRESERVE (which stands for Protecting the River Environment, Stopping Erosion, and Restoring the Vital Ecology), the students get their hands dirty removing nonnative Russian olive trees and Siberian elms. Sachi explains, "These invasive tree species absorb too much water and push out the native species such as the willows and cottonwoods. We have been lopping and spraying. However, instead of using environmentally harmful chemicals, our spray is made from vinegar and molasses. This slows growth and, after a few times, the spray gets into the roots and the nonnative plant dies."

The students also check water clarity, total dissolved solids, temperature, and pH, and test for copper, nitrates, and phosphates. For Sachi, the most important of these elements is phosphates—mineral deposits used as a fertilizer. The EPA phosphate standard for unpolluted water is 0.01 mg/l; just downstream from Santa Fe, phosphate is testing at a whopping 4.25 mg/l. Plants depend on phosphates to grow, but too many can cause eutrophication (chemical nutrient concentration). This leads to oxygen depletion, harms aquatic species, and threatens biodiversity. To make matters worse, decaying debris can build up in streambeds, converting rivers into swamps. Once this happens, there is no water source that people can use.

The class sought to participate in a State Water Commission Hearing. Could a group of teenage girls voice their opinions in government and be heard? "We decided to talk about phosphates because we knew about them," Sachi says. "We had presented to our school, knew the data, and even had made a short movie on the topic." The group asked the commission to consider establishing a standard for phosphates in the Santa Fe River. They also asked the commission to support a local ban on the sale of common household and industrial products that contain phosphates, including certain detergents.

On the day of the commission hearing, icy weather closed the schools in Santa Fe . . . and it was Sachi's birthday. "Our parents drove us to the capitol building, the Roundhouse. We walked into the building. Three of us were chosen to speak to the legislators: myself, Maddy, and Moriah. After being sworn in, we sat before the commission. In front of us was the board, plus a stenographer typing every word we spoke, and we testified—to add our voices to the record and influence public policy.

"A lot of kids think we can't change the world right now— but we really tried to change a law that would open eyes in other states as to how bad phosphates are for our environment. Phosphates are found in detergents and fertilizers we use every day. It takes so much money and energy to remove this in the wastewater plants. Instead, stop selling phosphates in products! We can find replacements, and if consumers demand different ingredients, then that's what will be manufactured. Right now, big companies are profiting in a way that hurts our economy and nature. Of course we have other planetary concerns—but remember, phosphates are a cause of eutrophication and that affects the web of life."

Next up—Sachi and the other students have been taking readings above the water treatment plant to identify the source of the phosphates in the Santa Fe River, and they will continue community involvement to ensure that young voices are heard.

# The Four Steps to Action

After reading this far, what's on your mind? Which concerns grab you the most? Perhaps a news headline sparked your thinking, or reading one of these Teens in Action! stories stirred up some ideas. Now is the time to really get your action on—and persuade others to join you—by following these four steps:

**Step 1:** Think about the needs in your community involving water directly, or any related topic that can affect our oceans and waterways.

**Step 2:** Consider what you know about this subject—the cause, and who is involved in the solution. Align yourself with partners or join people already in the process of improving what needs help.

**Step 3:** Find out more! Remember the tips on action research (pages 20–21) and use media, interviews, surveys, and your own observation and experience to increase what you know (rehearse your elevator speech!).

**Step 4:** Put your action plan on paper. List *who* will do *what* by *when*. Keep track of resources you need along the way.

## SPREAD THE LOVE!

Get out and enjoy the natural water resources our planet has to offer! Then, encourage others to do the same. People are more likely to protect what they know and love. If you live in the United States, visit one of the National Marine Sanctuaries: sanctuaries.noaa.gov. In Canada, visit Parks Canada: www.pc.gc.ca, and click on "National Marine Conservation Areas." For a worldwide list visit World Heritage at whc.unesco.org/en/list. You might also visit an aquarium in your area.

## Need More Ideas for Action?

### Tackle Trash:

- Pick up litter and dispose of it properly. (Remember: Debris in our waterways doesn't just fall from the sky; it falls from our own hands and eventually ends up in our lakes, rivers, and oceans.)

- Take your commitment year-round—join local beach, river, or stream cleanups.

- Use reusable cloth bags for groceries and shopping instead of disposable plastic bags.

- If you come across a plastic holder for a six-pack of cans or bottles, cut the plastic rings apart and dispose of them properly.

- Use reusable or biodegradable food and beverage containers rather than using Styrofoam or plastic containers.

- Reduce, Reuse, Recycle—and avoid products with excessive packaging.

- Talk "trash" with your friends and family—spread the word about the trashing of our waterways!

### Reduce Pollution:

- Use more efficient energy sources, such as compact fluorescent light bulbs.

- Turn off lights when you leave the room and be sure your electronics are turned off *and* unplugged.

- Know what goes down the drain. Remind family members to dispose of car oil, engine fluids, cleaners, medicines, or household chemicals in safe ways. Find approved motor oil and household chemical recycling or disposal facilities near your home and tell people about them.

*Vampire power* is the wasted use of energy by any electric appliances or gadgets that remain plugged in when not in use. An easy way to reduce vampire power is to connect all of your electronics to power strips that can be quickly turned on and off. You can also reduce general electricity waste by using electricity during off-peak hours.

**EARTHECHO**
INTERNATIONAL

# Write a Proposal

To be taken seriously in the world, putting your ideas into a written proposal lets people know that *you mean business*. Make that proposal, make it convincing, and get others involved.

Having a written proposal enables you also to share your plans with others. If you need permission to move your plan forward, perhaps from a teacher or principal, a proposal will help make it happen. A written document gives legitimacy to your idea when you want to involve people or groups as partners—be sure to clarify every partner's responsibilities and add it to the proposal. Often proposals are submitted to funders when money or supplies are needed to get the job done. Learning how to write a formal proposal will open many doors for you as you develop the skills to be a proponent for action.

What goes into your proposal? Here's a checklist of what typically is included—use the categories that match your situation.

- ☑ Names of Students and Adult Leaders

- ☑ Name of School or Organization

- ☑ Name of Action Plan

- ☑ Community Need (Why is this plan necessary?)

- ☑ Purpose (How will this plan meet the need?)

- ☑ Partners (Who else—individuals or organizations—will be involved?)

- ☑ Participation (Who will do what?)

- ☑ Outcomes (What do you expect to happen as a result of your efforts?)

- ☑ Evidence (How will you track the change being made?)

- ☑ Resources (What supplies or materials are required to get the job done?)

- ☑ Timeline (What will happen when?)

- ☑ Signatures of Participants

# Announce Your Plans

In addition to finding partners to help you take action, you might also find spectators. Publicize your plans for service and invite people from the community to observe, along with members of the media and local government. Put a spotlight on your act!

## Use the Media

The media can help you spread the news of your plans for action. As you develop your knowledge and gather resources, keep tabs on any local reporters or bloggers who regularly cover water and environment issues. Keep them posted as you make progress, and be sure to send a press release to every media outlet you can when the time for action arrives.

## Inform Policy Makers

Invite local, regional, or state leaders and influential people to observe or take part in your event or action. Give them plenty of notice ahead of time and send reminders as the event date approaches. Keep track of who the best contact person is in their offices and keep them posted on developments. Influencing our policy makers secures our future!

**Got Grants?**

Can young people get grants or funds to turn their ideas into realities? Absolutely! Many organizations look for good ideas from kids who have the desire, the ability, and the resolve to champion a cause and change the world for the better. Where to start? Visit Youth Service America, a national organization that lists many of these opportunities, at www.ysa.org.

# WRITING A PRESS RELEASE

The media want to know what you are planning and doing. If you have an event scheduled, alert the presses by creating a press release, which typically includes:

FOR IMMEDIATE RELEASE:
**Kids Storming for Clean Drains!**   *CATCHY TITLE*

*COMPELLING INFORMATION*

**September 10—Ocean City, California.**
We see this every day on the way to school—trash accumulated in the streets, entering the storm drains, and heading for the open waters.

*WHAT*

With permission and participation from City Council member T. Belle, over 50 dedicated members of Youth In Action and the City Council will clean the curbs along five miles of Mar Vista Avenue and stencil KEEP OUR SEAS SAFE reminders by each drain.   *WHO*

*WHEN*

**Date:** Tuesday, October 18
**Time:** 9 a.m. – 3 p.m.

*WHERE*

**Location:** Mar Vista Avenue from Ocean Park Boulevard to the coast.

For details, contact: Timothy Jones at 987-654-3210 or tjones@bluemail.com   *CONTACT INFORMATION*

Of course you can add more details than this in your press release, and still be brief, clear, and enticing to make sure the press covers your event. Be sure to follow up with phone call or email reminders. You can also send "press kits" to the media that include more information about your organization or project.

# Make Your Action Memorable

Get that camera poised to capture your success. Become a photojournalist and documentarian to catch the story as it unfolds. Scrapbook, anyone? If you like to cut and paste, save news articles, letters, photos of your activities, testimonials from friends who help out, and other pieces of your story and add them to the book.

Whether you choose to keep a journal, scrapbook, or Web page, remember to consistently capture the action all the way through so you can produce the visual story later. You may choose to include these visuals in a photomontage at a thank-you event with community partners, in an appreciation package that you send to funders, or in a proposal for your next action plan as proof that you accomplish what you set out to do. Be sure to tell it like it is—record the frustrations (they are inevitable) along with the *Hooray!* moments. This keeps the story authentic and serves as a helpful guide to others who may follow in your footsteps.

---

**Remember: Your Actions Matter.** Perhaps you were surprised or even amazed by some of the Kids in Action! stories in this book. Every single person who has made change happen in this world started with an idea and a question: "Can I really do this?" They discovered the answer: "Yes." And if they can, *you* can.

---

## Summary

**A**ction. Action is perhaps the most important stage on your service learning adventure, and you have made it count by investigating and preparing along the way. Whatever form your action takes—direct or indirect service, advocacy, or research—and whatever the results that occur, you have made your move toward going blue.

# STAGE 4
## THINK BACK→REFLECT

Do you sometimes press the pause button on a remote control or on your MP3 player to think about what you've just seen or heard? Reflection, the fourth stage on your service learning journey, is like that—it's a chance to pause and think about your experience from many angles, and also to learn from your slipups and successes.

# The Story of Tar Creek: Part #4
## Miami, Oklahoma, United States
(continued from page 102)

## How Did They Reflect?

"Have we made a change in the community?" Students continually consider the impact of their actions in various ways, always connecting their thoughts and feelings to the experience. Reflection happens through quiet moments, discussion, writing poetry, photography, and providing feedback to others that improves the ongoing work. All voices are welcome, all are heard.

> **Children have enough problems in the world—they do not need this lurking behind them, too. This is Mother Earth and we are supposed to take care of her and she will take care of us, but I think that we are severely slacking on our part.**
>
> —*Jessica Sage, Miami school student*

So after more than two decades as a Superfund site, has the Tar Creek area changed? Unfortunately—not enough. Even with the federal, state, county, city, and tribal governments involved, as well as the Environmental Protection Agency, Centers for Disease Control, and Harvard University . . . change is often slow.

## time for REFLECTION

Dangerous waters can be found in many places. Toxic sites will only increase unless we clean up our act. Your generation stands to inherit this problem. Talk about this with a friend, teacher, or family member. Who should be responsible for these messes? What can be done now?

*The Story of Tar Creek continues on page 132.*

# Pause, Look Back, & Reflect

All through *Going Blue* you've encountered Time for Reflection boxes that encouraged you to hit the pause button and consider, contemplate, ponder, digest, look back, and r-e-f-l-e-c-t. It's a good habit to adopt in all parts of your life. Just as water reflects our images back to us and lets us consider ourselves from a different perspective, taking time to reflect on our lives and our world helps us become more considerate of the environment that depends on us.

> "What are the best times to reflect on the course of your life? Whenever you are near water, such as the ocean, a quiet pond, or a small stream. Bodies of water help to stimulate your creative thought process."—Jeff Davidson, author of *Breathing Space*

# Here are some additional questions to help you flex your reflection muscles.

- Of all the Teens in Action! stories you read in this book, which one sticks in your head at this very moment? Why?

- Who is a likely partner for you in your *Going Blue* service learning plan? What will convince this person (or people) to get involved?

- Close your eyes and imagine our oceans and waterways being healthier. Picture sparkling blue water, swarms of colorful fish, vibrant coral reefs, pristine glacial lakes, clear deep rivers, and vast litter-free wetlands teeming with life. Which change would make you the most excited?

- How has learning about our oceans and waterways changed your daily habits or actions?

- A Sioux proverb reminds us that, "The frog does not drink up the pond in which he lives." What actions will you take to preserve our "pond" and keep this planet of ours healthy, dependable, and safe?

Think of a person you want to influence to go blue. Write a passionate statement that sums up your message, and come up with a memorable way to deliver your words (on a card shaped like a fish, perhaps?).

Our water systems frequently face threats—from overfishing to oil spills. Think of a recent incident, and compose your thoughts and feelings in a poem, song, rap, or comic strip. Then share with others.

Imagine the year is 2020. Reflect back on the changes you have seen on this water planet of ours. Journal about how *Going Blue* helped you to be a part of the solution.

Imagine that you are packing a suitcase for a trip, and you only have room for three words to take along that will be your reminders to go blue. Select with care. Pack them well. Share often.

What have you discovered about yourself on this journey?

## Summary

**R**eflection. To get where you're going in helping the world's waters, you have to know where you've been. Through reflection, you build wisdom and ensure that every lesson and insight is valued on this journey. Reflection keeps you on track, reminds you to think through each important decision, and brings to light the golden opportunities presented to you to better yourself and your world.

# STAGE 5
## TELL IT→DEMONSTRATE

By now you have taken some action . . . from saving water in your own home, to cutting water use at school, fighting runoff pollution, picking up trash along a beach, or helping repopulate a river with fish. Now is the time to shout your story from the rooftops—and the water towers! During Demonstration, the fifth stage of service learning, you will inform the world what you did, how you did it, who was involved, what you learned, and what the results were.

# The Story of Tar Creek: Part #5
## Miami, Oklahoma, United States
*(continued from page 126)*

## How Did They Demonstrate?

Change at Tar Creek may be slow, yet the students remain persistent. They keep writing books and hosting conferences. According to Rebecca Jim, who now devotes all her time to this effort through the L.E.A.D. agency:

> "Change is happening. It takes time and continued involvement of the citizens, the students, and in our case the states and the tribes. The government is people driven. Voices can be heard and in our case, children's voices. If these voices stop, the government's efforts can be diverted, since it is driven by what these voices say."

Miami students writing letters. Photo credit: Rebecca Jim

# The World Awaits: Tell Your Story

Here are some valuable tips on how to get in the papers (and on the computer screens), inform the community, and keep your voice echoing loud and clear.

Be **BOLD!** Stand up and tell your story.

**Know Your Audience.** Who will you tell your story to? The media, a business, the school board, a parent organization, younger students, politicians, a college class—be sure to frame the story you tell for your particular audience.

**Be Dynamic!** Use all your creative energy to make your show-and-tell as lively as possible. Avoid the typical "This is what we did" spiel, and instead:

- Use drama (act out penguins in peril).

- Create a mock game show (quiz the audience about ocean acidification).

- Do a choral reading (quite unexpected).

- Stage a surprise entrance with an alarming report and challenge the group to come up with solutions.

- Whatever you choose, engage your audience and challenge them to leave with at least one plan of action to improve our water environment.

**Inform Policy Makers . . . *Again!*** Did they show up when you did your action? If so, send them a huge THANKS! If they didn't show up, that's okay—send them photos, a video, or a collection of comments to show them how people got together in their community and took charge to make change. Then, perhaps next time you call for their attention, they'll answer readily.

# Once You Know It— Show It!

With all this expertise, now is the time for you to take the mantle of leadership. You can proudly and boldly become a spokesperson for our oceans and waterways. Picture it: Squads of cheerleading fish, dolphins, and jellies shouting, "Go, Team, Go!"

- Share what you know with others—kids and adults alike.
- Create a Going Blue club.
- Start a "Blue Blog."
- Write a comic book or graphic novel detailing your adventures.
- Make a film about your experience.
- Keep the adventure going.
- Become the eco-hero you were born to be.

## Summary

**Demonstration.** By demonstrating your service to others you've taken the crucial step to inform your community and the world about what can be done and what *is being* done to help save our oceans and waterways from distress. Demonstration will likely get others on board with you to help in future endeavors or guide them to begin service learning journeys of their own.

# What's Next?

Congratulations! You have completed your own service learning adventure.

Of course, this is truly only the beginning. Next, you can (and probably *will*—service is habit-forming) find ways to stay active and continue to apply your passions, skills, talents, and knowledge to protect our world for generations to come. Now it's your turn to venture downstream or offshore, seek out more Earth-saving adventures, and produce even more spectacular results.

EarthEcho International's **Water Planet Challenge** is a call-to-action that engages young people to protect and restore our water planet through service learning. Log onto www.waterplanetchallenge.org for tools and resources that you can use to stand up for a healthy future now. Joining the Water Planet Challenge will help you go blue and *stay* blue!

# Blue Books & Websites

You are definitely not floating alone out there. Check out these teen-friendly websites for ideas, information, and examples of what young people can do to go blue.

## Websites

EarthEcho International (www.earthecho.org) is a nonprofit organization that empowers young people to take action to protect and restore our water planet. EarthEcho inspires kids and teens to make global change by meeting local needs, helping them to understand the connections between community priorities and current critical ocean and water-related issues. The organization was founded by siblings Philippe and Alexandra Cousteau in honor of their father Philippe Cousteau Sr., son of the legendary explorer Jacques Cousteau.

H2O for Life (www.h2oforlifeschools.org) provides curriculum for schools to study the issues surrounding water in local communities as well as the global water crisis. Students learn how to be stewards of the earth while taking action to bring water, sanitation, and hygiene education to a global partner school in need.

Ocean Conservancy (www.oceanconservancy.org) promotes healthy and diverse ocean ecosystems, and opposes practices that threaten oceanic and human life. Its members advocate real leadership with cooperation among governments, businesses, scientists, policymakers, conservation organizations, and citizen activists. Together, they aim to create concrete solutions that lead to lasting change, so our oceans can be experienced for generations to come.

Save My Oceans (www.savemyoceans.com) is a company that entertains audiences first and then invites them to help make a difference. Save My Oceans is sponsored by Participant Media and has partnered with Disneynature and TakePart (www.TakePart.com). Visit their engaging website for ideas, information, and ways to get involved every day.

Your Environment, Your Choice (www.epa.gov/osw/education/teens) is a website provided by the U.S. Environmental Protection

Agency that invites teens to think, act, and find helpful resources regarding issues in the environment. Includes information about environmental careers.

# Books

*50 Ways to Save the Ocean* by David Helvarg (Inner Ocean Publishing, 2006). This well-researched book explores simple, everyday actions that protect and restore the ocean, from recycling plastic to buying locally grown produce. It also addresses issues of runoff pollution, wetland destruction, coral reef damage, and overfishing. Foreword by Philippe Cousteau.

> **"Three of my favorite books that address sustainability issues are *50 Ways to Save the Ocean* by David Helvarg, *Cradle to Cradle* by William McDonough & Michael Braungart, and the mother of all environmental books *Silent Spring* by Rachel Carson."**
> —Philippe Cousteau

*The Carbon Diaries, 2015* by Saci Lloyd (Holiday House, 2009). It's 2015 in London, England, and 15-year-old Laura is miserable, and she's keeping a diary. After a gigantic storm, the government has imposed carbon rationing and the whole world is watching. Gripping, relevant, and edgy. Also read the sequel: *The Carbon Diaries, 2017.*

*Cradle to Cradle: Remaking the Way We Make Things* by William McDonough & Michael Braungart (North Point Press, 2002). According to the authors of this book, most environmental pollution is the result of poor product design. Products can instead be designed to serve their function and, once discarded, to actually nourish the environment or provide high-quality materials for technical production. A manifesto of "eco-effectiveness."

*The Curse of Akkad: Climate Upheavals that Rocked Human History* by Peter Christie (Annick Press, 2008). Has climate change always affected our world? Yes. This book explains the relationship between climate and events like migration and war, from the days of Macedonia to witch hunts in Eastern Europe to Hitler's quest for power. Amazing true stories.

*Gone Fishing: Ocean Life by the Numbers* by David McLimans (Walker and Co., 2008). With its bright blue color reminiscent of ocean water, this counting book uses the shape of animals to count one to ten and back again. Each animal represents sea life threatened by human activity. With information, statistics, and resources, this book has something for everyone.

*Not a Drop to Drink: Water for a Thirsty World* by Michael Burgan (National Geographic, 2008). Using timelines, photographs, charts, and a glossary, this book explores a crucial issue: the need for clean, accessible water. Includes science (robotic sea-floor exploration), history (retrieving ocean fossils), current events (the war in Darfur), global awareness (world water consumption), and innovative ways this dilemma is being addressed (salt solutions).

*Protecting Earth's Water Supply* by Ron Fridell (Lerner Publications, 2008). Water, water everywhere? Not exactly. Human-induced pollution and global warming is threatening our water supply. Read about creative solutions for collecting water from fog and air, and how a 10-year-old from India developed a rainwater harvesting system to help local farmers.

*Scat* by Carl Hiaasen (Knopf, 2009). Nick and Marta should be relieved that Ms. Starch, the feared biology teacher, has gone missing after a field trip to Black Vine Swamp in the Florida Everglades. But something is amiss. Could Smoke, the class "delinquent," be behind this? What about the Florida panther on the prowl? Could a self-centered wannabe oilman be causing these problems? This eco-thriller is a real page-turner.

*Silent Spring* by Rachel Carson (Mariner Books, 2002). First published in 1962, this landmark book alerted a large audience to the environmental and human dangers of careless use of pesticides, spurring revolutionary changes in the laws affecting our air, land, and water.

# Afterword
## for Teachers, Youth Leaders, Parents, & Other Adults

### Use This Book to Inspire Young Activists

Teens have ideas, energy, and enthusiasm that can benefit our communities once they get involved. The question may be, where to start? By giving this book to students or to your own children, you are helping them participate successfully in service learning. The process of completing the activities helps them develop personal skills, knowledge, and abilities required to address the community needs they care about. Teens can use this book themselves, or adults can guide them in its use in school, youth groups, or a family setting. The following sections explain in more detail how these groups can get the most out of this guide.

*Please note:* While some consider the topics of climate change and global warming to be controversial, this book relies on the general consensus from the international scientific community that it is a fact.

### In a School Setting

This book can easily be used in various ways within a school:

**Academic Class:** As part of a unit of study about the planet's water system—whether local, national, or international—this book provides an interdisciplinary approach to examining this important issue. Students look at issues from various perspectives, analyze information, conduct research, read an interview with an expert, discuss others' service efforts, develop activity plans, and put their plans into action. The book's activities can be implemented over three to six weeks of class time when used continuously, depending on the length of the service experience. Another option is to complete one to two activities per week and extend the study over a semester.

**Advisory Class:** Many schools have a dedicated 30- to 40-minute weekly advisory class meant to improve academic skills, provide opportunities for social-emotional development, and allow for a successful experience in a course of study or exploration. This book helps students develop communication and research skills, teamwork, and problem solving, while working to make a significant contribution. When implemented in a weekly advisory class, all the activities could be completed in about three months.

**After-School Program:** These varied activities suit an after-school program. They are easily implemented and include many creative opportunities for expression that vary the teaching and learning methods. Different ages of students also can collaborate successfully. Activities can be completed in partner work as well as small and large group experiences. If implemented twice a week in an after-school program, the activities would most likely extend over three months.

**Student Council:** If you are looking for a way to transform a typical student council community service project into a service learning experience, this book can be your guide. As students are exploring the issues, they can develop a service plan that extends into the student body. Part of the plan could be an awareness campaign with the leadership students sharing with fellow students what they consider to be the most important information in this book, augmented by what they discover through research.

## Words of Advice from the Field

Florida state award-winning teacher David Makepeace offers advice for teachers just starting out with service learning:

- Lean heavily on your students and their interests.
- Take advantage of local resources, including people and service learning opportunities. Seek assistance from experienced service learning practitioners.
- Pay as much (or more) attention to the learning as to the service.
- Realize that no project is too small and it is better to start small and build on success.
- Make sure you thoroughly investigate community partners.
- Get the support of your school administration.
- Have your students document what they do and let your community know about the successes.
- Remember, it is about the *students*.
- And finally: Have fun!

## In Youth Groups

As service learning grows in popularity with youth groups, program staff often looks for activities that encourage academic skills in a nontraditional manner. Use of this book is most effective when consistent—for example, one or two times per week—so students know what to expect and what is expected of them. The activities compiled here offer opportunities for lively discussion, firsthand community experiences, creative expression (for example, writing, poetry, drama, and art), and integrated reflection.

## As a Family

Family service projects provide opportunities for common exploration and experience. Rather than emphasizing the academic elements, families can use the book to guide them through the terrain of the service learning process while gaining collective knowledge and stimulating ideas for service plans. It's helpful for family members to approach investigating this topic on equal ground, with the youngest members being encouraged to share their thoughts and ideas.

For every participant, this book is designed to open minds, create possibilities, and encourage the lasting benefits that occur when making a contribution of one's personal talents and skills. Each person has value in the service learning process.

*Cathryn Berger Kaye, M.A.*

# Sources for Blue Facts

What Do You Know?

The Canadian Press. "Human Overfishing Starves Dolphins, Sharks, Seabirds: Study." *The Canadian Press*. March 2, 2009.

National Oceanic and Atmospheric Administration. "State of the Climate Global Analysis 2009." National Climatic Data Center, United States Department of Commerce.

STAGE 1: Find Out→Investigate
*The Story of Tar Creek: Parts #1–5*
L.E.A.D. Agency, Inc. "Facts." (www.leadagency.org/Facts.html)

You're All Wet!
Alter, Alexandra. "Yet Another 'Footprint' to Worry About: Water: Taking a Cue from Carbon Tracking, Companies and Conservationists Tally Hidden Sources of Consumption." *The Wall Street Journal*. February 17, 2009.

Water Footprint Network. "Water Footprint Product Gallery." (www.waterfootprint.org/?page=files/productgallery)

U.S. Geological Society. "Water Science for Schools: Water Q & A: Water Use at Home." (ga.water.usgs.gov/edu/qahome.html)

The American Water Works Association (AWWA). "55 Facts, Figures & Follies of Water Conservation." Denver Water Department, Denver, CO. 2001.

Washington Suburban Sanitary Commission. "Water Usage Chart." (www.wssc.dst.md.us/service/WaterUsageChart.cfm)

Human Development Report Office. "Human Development Report 2006: Beyond Scarcity: Power, Poverty and the Global Water Crisis." United Nations Development Programme.

Water, Water, Everywhere . . . or Is It?
National Marine Sanctuaries. "Education." (sanctuaries.noaa.gov/education)

The MarineBio Conservation Society. "Ocean Facts." (www.marinebio.org/MarineBio/Facts)

Save the Sea. "Interesting Ocean Facts." (www.savethesea.org/STS ocean_facts)

Community Water Needs
*Potable Water*
Human Development Report Office. "Human Development Report 2006: Beyond Scarcity: Power, Poverty and the Global Water Crisis." United Nations Development Programme.

Mundra, Raj. "Does Community Service Really Change Anything: Our Group of Teens Discovered the Answer Is Complex." *The Christian Science Monitor.* December 29, 2008.

*Water Privatization*
FLOW: How Did a Handful of Corporations Steal Our Water? "About Water." (www.flowthefilm.com/aboutwater)

Water.org. "Water Facts." (water.org/learn-about-the-water-crisis/facts)

Royte, Elizabeth. *Bottlemania: Big Business, Local Springs, and the Battle Over America's Drinking Water.* New York: Bloomsbury Publishing, 2009.

Whiteley, John M., Helen Ingram, and Richard Warren Perry, eds. *Water, Place, & Equity.* Cambridge: Massachusetts Institute of Technology, 2008.

Center for Global Policy. School of Public Policy, George Mason University. (globalpolicy.gmu.edu)

The Carter Center. (www.cartercenter.org)

Global Policy Forum. "Water in Conflict." (www.globalpolicy.org/security-council/dark-side-of-natural-resources/water-in-conflict.html)

*Bottled Water*
Tappening. "Why Not Bottled Water?" (www.tappening.com/Why_Not_Bottled_Water)

AllAboutWater.org. "The Effects of Bottled Water on the Environment." (www.allaboutwater.org/environment.html)

Clark Howard, Brian. "Message in a Bottle: Despite the Hype, Bottled Water Is Neither CLEANER nor GREENER Than Tap Water." *E: The Environmental Magazine* 14, no. 5 (September/October 2003).

Hoffman, Sue. "Students Tap Into Bottle-Waste Stream." *Chagrin Valley Times.* April 29, 2009.

The Container Recycling Institute. "Bottled Water." (www.container-recycling.org/issues/bottledwater.htm)

*Where's the Water in Your Backyard?*
United States Environmental Protection Agency. "What Is a Watershed?" (www.epa.gov/owow/watershed/whatis.html)

*Your Piece of the Watershed*
*Rivers and Creeks*
American Rivers. *America's Most Endangered Rivers: 2009 Edition.* Washington, DC: American Rivers, 2009.

Wong, C.M., J. Pittock, U. Collier, and P. Schelle. *World's Top 10 Rivers at Risk.* Gland, Switzerland: World Wild Life International, March 2007.

*Estuaries*
Office of Naval Research: Science & Technology Focus. "Oceanography." "Habitats." (www.onr.navy.mil/focus/ocean/habitats)

Laffoley, Dan, and Gabriel Grimsditch, eds. *The Management of Natural Coastal Carbon Sinks.* Gland, Switzerland: International Union for Conservation of Nature and Natural Resources, 2009.

Hoyle, Brian. "Bioaccumulation." JRank.org. (science.jrank.org/pages/854/Bioaccumulation.html)

*Lakes*
Ishii, Satoshi, Dennis L. Hansen, Randall E. Hicks, and Michael J. Sadowsky. "Beach Sand and Sediments Are Temporal Sinks and Sources of *Escherichia coli* in Lake Superior." *Environmental Science & Technology* 41 no. 7 (2007): 2203–2209.

Dorfman, Mark, and Kirsten Sinclair Rosselot. *Testing the Waters: A Guide to Water Quality at Vacation Beaches.* New York: The Natural Resources Defense Council, 2009.

*Coastal Areas*
Office of Naval Research: Science & Technology Focus. "Oceanography." "Habitats." (www.onr.navy.mil/focus/ocean/habitats)

Diaz, Robert J., and Rutger Rosenberg. "Spreading Dead Zones and Consequences for Marine Ecosystems." *Science* 321 (2008): 926–929.

## STAGE 2: Dive In→Prepare

The Amazing Ocean

National Marine Sanctuaries. "Education." (sanctuaries.noaa.gov/education)

National Oceanic and Atmospheric Administration. "Ocean." United States Department of Commerce. (www.noaa.gov/ocean.html)

The Carbon Conundrum: Part #1—Ocean Acidification

The Natural Resources Defense Council. "Ocean Acidification: The Other CO2 Problem." (www.nrdc.org/oceans/acidification)

Sabine, Christopher L., Richard A. Feely, Nicolas Gruber, Robert M. Key, Kitack Lee, John L. Bullister, Rik Wanninkhof, et. al. "The Oceanic Sink for Anthropogenic CO2." *Science* 305 (2004): 367–371.

*Food Chain, Interrupted*

Sample, Ian. "Unexpected Rise in Carbon-Fuelled Ocean Acidity Threatens Shellfish, Say Scientists." *The Guardian.* November 25, 2008.

McKie, Robin. "Artic Seas Turn to Acid, Putting Vital Food Chain at Risk." *The Guardian*, October 4, 2009.

The Carbon Conundrum: Part #2—Climate Change

Gagosian, Robert B. *Abrupt Climate Change: Should We Be Worried?* Woods Hole, MA: The Woods Hole Oceanographic Institution, 2003.

*The Global Conveyor Belt*

National Oceanic and Atmospheric Administration. "The Global Conveyor Belt." United States Department of Commerce. (oceanservice.noaa.gov/education/kits/currents/06conveyor3.html)

*"I'm Melting!"*

Myers, Steven Lee, Andrew C. Revkin, Simon Romero, and Clifford Krauss. "Old Ways of Life Are Fading as the Arctic Thaws." *The New York Times*. October 20, 2005.

Windows to the Universe. "Warming of the Polar Regions." University Corporation for Atmospheric Research. (www.windows.ucar.edu/tour/link=/earth/polar/polar_climate.html)

Marian Koshland Science Museum of the National Academy of Sciences. "Amplifiers: Ice-Reflectivity Feedback." (www.koshland-science-museum.org/exhibitgcc/causes13.jsp)

Windows to the Universe. "The Cryosphere and Global Climate Change." University Corporation for Atmospheric Research. (www.windows.ucar.edu/tour/link=/earth/polar/cryosphere_climate1.html)

Hu, Aixue, Gerald Meehl, Weiqing Han, and Jianjun Yin. "Transient Response of the MOC and Climate to Potential Melting of the Greenland Ice Sheet in the 21st Century." *Geophysical Research Letters*. May 27, 2009.

Plastics, Pollution, & Trash

Ocean Conservancy, Inc. "Ocean Conservancy: Start a Sea Change." (www.oceanconservancy.org)

Greenpeace. "Oceans." (www.greenpeace.org/usa/campaigns/oceans)

*The Great Pacific Garbage Patch*

Cava, Marco R. "Birds, Boats Threatened by Great Garbage Patch." *USA Today*. November 16, 2009, Life Section.

Greenberg, Paul. "The Oceans' Junkyards (a review of *Flotsametrics and the Floating World: How One Man's Obsession with Runaway Sneakers and Rubber Ducks Revolutionized Ocean Science* by Curtis Ebbesmeyer and Eric Scigliano). *The New York Times Book Review*. May 14, 2009.

McNally, Shelagh. "Searching for a 'Green Plastic' Solution," *Financial Post* (Canada). May 29, 2009.

Biodegradable Products Institute, Inc. "The Compostable Label." (www.bpiworld.org/BPI-Public/Program.html)

Basu, Saikat. "The Largest 'Landfill' on Earth; the Great Pacific Garbage Patch." *Digital Journal*. July 28, 2008.

*Runoff Pollution*
National Oceanic & Atmospheric Administration. "International Year of the Ocean—Kids' & Teachers' Resources." (www.yoto98.noaa.gov/kids.htm)

Coral Reefs in Crisis
Office of Naval Research: Science & Technology Focus. "Oceanography." "Habitats." (www.onr.navy.mil/focus/ocean/habitats)

Looking Back: Historical Moments & Actions
*A Brief History of Ocean Exploration*
McLaughlin, Charles H., Jr. "Our Blue Planet: Ocean Exploration." *Technology and Children*. December 1, 2005.

*Animal Lifeguards: Eugenia Clark & Archie Carr*
Krueger, Curtis. "Curiosity Drove Her to Become 'Shark Lady'." *St. Petersburg Times*. March 18, 2006.

Ehrenfeld, David. M.D. "Archie Carr Tribute." The Caribbean Conservation Corporation. (cccturtle.org/aboutccc.php?page=carr)

STAGE 3: Get Going→Act!
Your Little Choices Make a Big Splash
"Pollution Prevention (P2) Education Toolbox: Tools for Helping Teachers Integrate P2 Concepts in the Classroom." United States Environmental Protection Agency. EPA-905-F-97-011. August, 1997.

Earth 911. "E-waste: Harmful Materials." (earth911.com/electronics/e-waste-harmful-materials)

Farming & Food
Marks, Susan J. *Aqua Shock: The Water Crisis in America*. New York: Bloomburg Press, 2009.

Overfishing
Greenpeace. "Oceans." (www.greenpeace.org/usa/campaigns/oceans)

Take Action
Ocean Conservancy, Inc. (www.oceanconservancy.org)

Greenpeace. (www.greenpeace.org)

National Oceanic and Atmospheric Administration. United States Department of Commerce. (www.noaa.gov)

United States Environmental Protection Agency. (www.epa.gov)

# Index